MANAGING CORPORATE TURNAROUND

By the same author:

Financial Ratios and The Prediction of Corporate Failure

Management and Monitoring of Industrial Sickness
(*Won the DMA-ESCORTS* **Best Book Award 1986**)

Managing Corporate Turnaround

(Text and Cases)

R.A. YADAV
Faculty of Management Studies
University of Delhi, Delhi

CONCEPT PUBLISHING COMPANY, NEW DELHI 110059

ISBN 81-7022-419-5

First Published 1992

Published and Printed by
Ashok Kumar Mittal
Concept Publishing Company
A/15-16, Commercial Block, Mohan Garden
NEW DELHI 110059 (India)

Lasertypeset by
Microtech Advance Printing Systems (Pvt.) Ltd.
H-13, Bali Nagar
NEW DELHI 110015

PREFACE

Industrial sickness is an alarmingly growing phenomenon of the Indian economy. It has been affecting the health of industrial units of all types, sizes and in all regions of the country and has assumed serious dimensions in recent years. There were 2,42,584 sick industrial units involving an outstanding bank credit of Rs. 7705.30 crores as at the end of December 1988. The locked up capital in sick industrial units may exceed Rs. 10,000 crores if rescheduling of payment is considered as inability to meet the obligations in time. About 44 per cent of the Central Government public sector enterprises are loss making and a significantly higher percentage of states enterprises are also running is losses. Data are not available how many industrial units are prone to sickness. If statistics are worked out on some criterion of industrial unit being prone to sickness, it is likely to indicate that industrial sickness has been growing at alarming rate and its rise seems to be unabated.

Apart from the loss and mental pain to the entrepreneurs, managers, employees and their families, the economy as whole is adversely affected by industrial sickness since it ties up vast public funds, accelerate industrial sickness, dampen the spirit of entrepreneurship and slows down the industrial growth. No doubt, a large number of measures have been initiated by the Government, Reserve Bank of India, Commercial banks and financial institutions for the revival of sick industrial units. They have been striving hard and spending a sizeable amount of resources to combat it. The enactment of Sick Industrial Companies Act, 1985 (SICA), setting up the Board of Industrial and Financial Reconstruction (BIFR) and the adoption of the Bill empowering BIFR to consider cases of sick public sector undertakings in 1991 are some of the major steps in this direction. However, they have not made much dent. Hence, it is a matter of grave concern that is reflected in the various statements made at the highest levels in Government and the Parliament. Keeping in view the progressive increase in industrial sickness and the results of various steps initiated to stem it, there is need for a more systematic approach to deal with specific issues relating to the problem of industrial sickness and turnaround management:

(i) Why do some running companies fall sick, while others thrive?
(ii) Can the on-set of sickness be predicted? If yes, when and how to detect it?
(iii) Is the industrial sickness beyond control? If no, how to prevent it?
(iv) Can the sick industrial units be turned around? If yes, what turnaround strategies are to be initiated, when and how? What role does top management play in turning around sick units?

The first three issues are covered in detail is my earlier books namely *Financial Ratios and the Prediction of Corporate Failure* and *Management and Monitoring of Industrial Sickness*. It is clearly pointed out that the detection of sickness is possible as early as 6 years in advance. Keeping the dictum '*prevention is better than cure*' in mind, preventive measures have also been suggested. My interest in the subject has been sustained over the years and the present book which discusses in detail the various aspects of the fourth issue i.e. managing corporate turnaround, is in continuation of my earlier work. It is an attempt to have better understanding of why running units fall sick and how can they be turned around successfully. In a nation of rampant industrial sickness and resource crunch like India, a better understanding of corporate decline and turnaround management becomes all the more important. The book explores the dynamics of corporate decline and turnaround mechanisms which should be of great help to the owners, managements, banks, financial institutions and government in turning around the sick industrial units. It is clearly pointed out that the effective management can turnaround the sick units successfully even in adverse circumstances.

The book is presented in two parts. Part I contains four chapters which are devoted to the dynamics of decline, turnaround stages and strategies thereon, turnaround requirements and monitoring performance. When and how to diagnose and predict the onset of sickness including MDA model is also dealt with in the first chapter. Part II discusses six Indian case studies of successful turnarounds. The purpose of presenting the case studies of successful turnaround is to learn how the ailing industrial units can be successfully turnedaround and draw lessons from the turnaround mechanisms used by them for the future. It is hoped that the book would prove useful to the managers of industries, funding institutions and government in assessing the state of health of sick industrial units and formulating effective turnaround strategies for them.

I express my deep sense of gratitude to Prof. T.N. Kapoor, Vice-Chancellor, Panjab University, Chandigarh, for the guidance and encouragement in completing the work in time. I am also grateful to Prof. B.C. Tandon, ex-Dean. Faculty of Management Studies, Prof. B.S. Sharma, former Pro-Vice-Chancellor, Indira Gandhi National Open University, Prof M.P. Gupta, Dean, Faculty of Management Studies, University of Delhi and Prof. Mohinder N. Kaura, Administrative Staff College of India, Hyderabad for their stimulating comments and fruitful discussions. My friends Prof. Chetan Baxi, Management Development Institute Gurgaon, Dr. P.C. Jain, Reader, Shri Ram College of Commerce and Dr. G.L. Sharma, Reader, Deshbandhu College, University of Delhi, deserve a special mention for their interest evinced in the study and discussion held from time to time. Most of the data for case studies has been culled from information widely scattered in the periodicals. The references in the book are only a modest acknowledgement of my debt to other writers. I also express my thanks to the participants in various training programmes who sharpened and refined my understanding of the subject both in regard to its relevance and limitations.

Finally, credit is also due to my wife Shyama, Son, Nishant and daughter, Shivani for their patience, understanding and loving support while this book was in preparation. I will feel gratified if the book is found useful to the managers and also to researchers in this important area of industrial sickness and turnaround management.

R.A. YADAV

CONTENTS

LIST OF TABLES

LIST OF FIGURES

PART I

TEXT

1

THE DYNAMICS OF CORPORATE DECLINE

The spectrum of industries in India extends from the organised large and medium scale units to small scale units which constitute an important segment of the economy. It is fortunate that the nation-builders of India had the vision to give the industrial sector the high priority it deserves, as they knew that the economic growth with stability would depend to a large extent on the profitability and financial soundness of this sector. However, industrial sickness, of late, has been afflicting the health of units of all types, sizes and in all regions. It may be admitted that when industrial units are promoted on a gigantic scale, some units are bound to awary, but it needs to be kept as low a limit as possible to sustain industrial growth.

The failure of a business unit is an event which brings a lot of mental pain to the entrepreneurs, managers, employees and their families. The economy as a whole is adversely affected by industrial sickness as unemployment goes up, availability of goods and services decreases and their cost goes up, ties up vast public funds, makes banks and financial institutions sick, accelerates massive industrial unrest, slows down industrial growth rate and generally dampens the spirit of entrepreneurship. The investors lose their savings and creditors lose their cash and future business. The growth of those units which depend on sick units for raw material, finished goods etc. is also affected adversely. Thus, a coherent framework setting out the dynamics of corporate decline, detecting it on time and better understanding of preventive measures and managing turnaround of sick units is the need of the hour. Such a coherent and systematic knowledge about corporate decline and managing its turnaround would help the management to monitor the health of enterprise more effectively, provide banks, financial institutions and the government with pragmatic alternatives to the current ineffective ways of dealing with growing incidence of industrial sickness and serve to minimise, if not eliminate such losses by providing ample warning in advance to those concerned. Keeping the above in view, an attempt has been made in this direction in this book.

DIMENSIONS OF INDUSTRIAL SICKNESS

The problem of industrial sickness has become a world-wide phenomenon. In the U.K. over 10,000 units are estimated to fail each year and, one out of five firms listed on the stock exchanges turns sick (Slatter, 1984, p. 18) and of these only one in four manages a successful turnaround. During the decade, 1967-76, one in four companies listed on the U.S. Stock exchanges had turned sick and only one-third of them got recovered (Bibeault, 1982). West Germany, once acclaimed the locomotive economy of Europe, alone reported over 12000 bankruptcies in 1982 (*The Economic Times*, February 10, 1986). The death toll of industries in developing countries like India has been more alarming. Banks once the citadels of commercial credit, have now become the intensive care centres for critically and terminally sick industrial units.

In India, growing phenomenon of industrial sickness has been one of the persisting problems. Industrial sickness, with in large and small scale industry, has assumed serious dimensions in recent years. It has affected industries of all types, sizes and in all regions of the country. Substantial amount of loanable funds of the banks and financial institutions is locked up in sick industrial units, causing not only wastage of resources but also affecting the healthy growth of the economy. It has been a matter of grave concern for banks and financial institutions because of its far-reaching implications for the entire economy and the industrial sector in particular. As at the end of December 1988 as per the latest data available (*Economic Survey, 1990-91*), there were 2,42,584 sick industrial units on the portfolios of scheduled commercial banks and financial institutions involving an outstanding bank credit of Rs. 7705.30 crores which was about 9.8 per cent of the total outstanding bank credit. The break-up in respect of SSI sick units, non-SSI sick units (covered by SICA, 1985), non-SSI weak units (not covered by SICA) and the amount blocked in each is given in Table 1.1. The analysis of Table 1.1 reveals that between end-December 1986 and end-December 1987 and end-December 1988, the number of sick units had gone up by 39.5 per cent and 17.7

TABLE 1.1: Industrial Sickness

Category	No. of Units			Amount Outstanding (Rs. Crores)		
	End December 1986	End December 1987	End December 1988	End December 1986	End December 1987	End December 1988
1	2	3	4	5	6	7
1. SSI Sick Units	145776 (21.9)	204259 (40.1)	240573 (17.8)	1306.10 (22.0)	1797.31 (37.6)	2141.00 (19.1)
2. Non-SSI Sick Units (covered by SICA 1985)	1964 (7.7)	1119 (−43.0)	1241 (10.9)	3568.39 (11.5)	2801.79 (−21.5)	3387.30 (20.9)
3. Non-SSI Weak Units (not covered by SICA 1985)	—	720	770 (6.9)	—	1657.30	2177.00 (31.4)
Total	147740 (23.5)	206098 (39.5)	242584 (17.7)	4874.49 (14.1)	6256.40 (28.3)	7705.30 (23.2)

Note: Figures in parentheses indicate the percentage change over the previous year.
Source: *Economic Survey, 1990-91* p. 52.

per cent and the bank credit outstanding against these units by 28.3 per cent and 23.2 per cent respectively. It further indicates that sickness has been growing faster in the small scale sector than in the large and medium scale sectors in terms of number of units, but it was faster in the non-SSI sector in terms of outstanding bank credit. More then 72 per cent of the bank credit outstanding was locked up in the accounts of the non-SSI sick and weak industrial units as on end-December 1988. As per RBI data, out of 22.47 lakhs borrowal accounts in the SSI sector as on 31st December, 1987, 2.04 lakhs were reported to be sick, which means that every eleventh SSI unit in the country was sick. There has been a constant increase in the number of industrial units going into liquidation and also those taken over by the government for rehabilitation.

The locked up capital in sick industrial units today may exceed Rs. 10,000 crores if rescheduling of payment is also considered as a sign of inability to meet the obligation in time. Apart from bank funds, the public sector financial institutions funds are also blocked in sick industrial units. In one single year, the arrears of the dues of financial institutions outstanding from the sick units went up from Rs. 150 crores to Rs. 595 crores by the end of December 1984. Besides these, many of the public sector enterprises covering an immense variety of sizes, technologies and products are sick. About 44 per cent of the Central Government public sector enterprises are loss making and a significantly higher percentage of states-owned enterprises are also loss making. Over the last four decades there has been phenomenal increase in the size of Central public sector enterprises in terms of number and investment. Its size grew from a mere 5 enterprises as on 1-4-1951 to 244 enterprises as on 31-3-1990 with an investment of Rs. 29 crores to Rs. 99,315 crores respectively. Of these there were 106 and 98 sick units incurring a loss of Rs. 1923.21 crores and Rs. 1959.09 crores during 1988-89 and 1989-90 respectively. And Forty-five units have been identified by the Bureau of Public Enterprises (BPE) as non-viable. Table 1.2 shows the percentage of loss-making Public Enterprises to total operating Public Enterprises attached to the Central Government for the period 1969-70 to 1989-90. Only the operational enterprises have been taken into account for this purpose. The data availability position regarding industrial sickness is far from satisfactory. No statistics are available on how many industrial units both private and public sector, are prone to sickness. The data compiled by Reserve

Bank of India do not indicate the actual or the likely loss of employment and output arising out of the sickness of industrial units. If statistics were worked out on some criterion of an industrial unit being prone to sickness, it would indicate that industrial sickness has been growing at an alarming rate and the rise of it seems to be unabated.

TABLE 1.2: Sickness in Public Sector

Year	No. of Operating Enterprises	No of Loss-making Enterprises	Percentage Reporting losses	Losses of Loss-making Enterprises (Rs. Crores)	Net Post-tax Profit/Loss of all Public Enterprises (Rs. Crores)
1969-70	73	32	44	−75.7	−3.4
1972-73	101	34	34	−86.7	18.0
1975-76	121	34	28	−126.0	29.1
1978-79	159	68	43	−516.7	−40.1
1980-81	168	74	44	−760.1	−202.9
1981-82	188	83	44	−847.0	445.9
1982-83	193	82	43	−982.6	613.5
1983-84	201	92	46	−1537.8	240.1
1984-85	207	92	44	−1111.9	908.9
1985-86	211	90	43	−1684.2	1172.4
1986-87	214	100	47	−1706.5	1771.4
1987-88	220	103	47	−1745.0	2030.5
1988-89	226	106	47	−1923.2	2993.5
1989-90	233	98	42	−1959.1	3781.7

Source: Public Enterprises Survey, 1989-90, Vol. I, Ch. I.

Industrywise and Statewise Incidence of Sickness

The industrywise and statewise break-up of non-SSI sick units (covered by SICA, 1985) given in Table 1.3 indicates that statewise sickness was highest in Maharashtra (252), followed by West Bengal (151), Gujarat (131), Tamil Nadu (107), Andhra Pradesh (70), Uttar Pradesh (68), Karnataka (62) and so on. These seven states accounted for 75.2 per cent of the total number of non-SSI sick units and 79.4 per cent of the total outstanding bank credit as at end-December 1987. Industrywise classification indicates that sickness was highest in the case of engineering units (249), followed by textile (224) and chemicals (118). These three industry groups accounted for 52.8 per cent of the total number of non-SSI sick units and 62 per cent of the total outstanding bank credit as at end-December 1987.

The industrywise and statewise classification of non-SSI weak industrial units (not covered by SICA, 1985) is given in Table 1.4. There were 720 non-SSI weak industrial units with an outstanding bank credit of Rs. 1657.30 crores as at end-December 1987. Statewise, the number of non-SSI weak units was largest in Maharashtra (144), followed by West Bengal (119), Uttar Pradesh (64), Gujarat (58), etc. Industrywise, the sickness was more rampant in the case of textiles (160) and engineering (141). The incidence of sickness in small scale sector continued to be high. The number of SSI Sick units increased by 40 per cent and bank credit outstanding against these units rose by 37.6 per cent between December 1986 and December 1987. Statewise classification in Table 1.5 shows that at the end of December 1987, the bank credit outstanding against SSI sick units was the highest for Maharashtra (Rs. 331.72 crores), followed by Tamil Nadu (Rs. 193.15 crores), West Bengal (Rs. 182.32 crores), Uttar Pradesh (Rs. 148.03 crores), Andhra Pradesh (Rs. 138.48 crores) etc. The number of SSI sick units was highest in Tamil Nadu (30942) followed by West Bengal (21409), Uttar Pradesh (19710), Andhra Pradesh (19206), Maharashtra (15401), Kerala (1506) etc. as at the end of December 1987.

NEED FOR A CONTROLLING MECHANISM

The progressive increase in industrial sickness has been a matter of grave concern for banks, financial institutions and government on account of its far-reaching implications for the entire economy and the industrial sector in particular. A developing country like India experiencing shortage of several products, constraints of resources and mounting unemployment can ill-afford the growing incidence of industrial sickness as the common effects of sickness are locking up of financial resources, wastage of capital assets, loss of production, decrease in employment and massive industrial unrest. No doubt, a large number of measures have been initiated at the macro level by the government, Reserve Bank of India, commercial banks and financial institutions for the revival of sick industrial units as well as to prevent the increasing incidence of industrial sickness (Srivastava and Yadav, 1986, pp. 195-264 and Appendix). The government,

TABLE 1.3: State-wise and Industry-wise Classification of Non-SSI Sick Industrial Units and Outstanding Bank Credit as at the end of December 1987

(Rupees in crores)

State/Union Territories	Engineering		Electrical		Textiles		Jute		Paper		Rubber	
	No. of units	Amount out-standing	No. of units	Amount out-standing	No. of units	Amount out-standing	No. of units	Amount out-standing	No. of units	Amount out-standing	No. of units	Amount out-standing
1	2	3	4	5	6	7	8	9	10	11	12	13
Assam	1	0.29	—	—	—	—	—	—	3	7.01	—	—
Meghalaya	—	—	—	—	—	—	—	—	—	—	—	—
Mizoram	—	—	—	—	—	—	—	—	—	—	—	—
Bihar	3	8.03	—	—	3	2.59	—	—	3	3.77	—	—
West Bengal	40	146.59	2	2.03	13	23.87	32	112.99	9	26.06	1	7.23
Orissa	1	0.11	—	—	1	4.57	—	—	1	9.45	—	—
Tripura	—	—	—	—	—	—	—	—	—	—	—	—
Uttar Pradesh	9	23.96	2	0.89	9	45.77	—	—	8	7.54	—	—
Delhi	5	10.82	—	—	3	7.09	—	—	5	7.20	—	—
Punjab	5	1.55	—	—	7	2.25	—	—	2	4.01	—	—
Haryana	13	27.86	—	—	7	10.03	—	—	2	1.60	—	—

(Contd.)

TABLE 1.3 (*Contd.*)

1	2	3	4	5	6	7	8	9	10	11	12	13
Chandigarh	4	7.94	1	5.14	3	8.51	—	—	5	10.29	—	—
Jammu & Kashmir	—	—	—	—	—	—	—	—	—	—	—	—
Himachal Pradesh	1	0.28	—	—	—	—	—	—	2	0.62	—	—
Rajasthan	5	3.74	1	9.41	14	25.50	—	—	6	5.36	—	—
Gujarat	27	44.86	1	0.37	52	237.30	—	—	7	24.72	—	—
Maharashtra	69	206.92	3	7.10	60	263.00	—	—	9	9.80	7	17.49
Goa	2	2.22	—	—	1	0.50	—	—	—	—	—	—
Dadra & Nagar Haveli	—	—	—	—	—	—	—	—	—	—	—	—
Madhya Pradesh	6	4.49	1	1.79	8	59.00	—	—	3	1.43	1	0.33
Andhra Pradesh	14	17.09	2	3.59	4	20.42	1	0.89	7	8.19	1	0.98
Karnataka	15	32.16	—	—	11	33.02	—	—	7	9.02	2	2.09
Tamil Nadu	25	55.04	1	1.42	24	84.93	1	0.03	7	7.51	2	0.97
Kerala	2	41.33	1	2.43	4	19.88	—	—	—	—	2	41.46
Pondicherry	2	0.93	—	—	—	—	—	—	1	1.66	—	—
Total	249	636.21	15	34.17	224	948.23	34	113.91	87	145.24	16	70.55

(*Contd.*)

TABLE 1.3 (*Contd.*)

(*Rupees in crores*)

State/Union Territories	Cement		Iron & Steel		Sugar		Chemicals		Miscellaneous		Total	
	No. of units	Amount out-standing	No. of units	Amount out-standing	No. of units	Amount out-standing	No. of units	Amount out-standing	No. of units	Amount out-standing	No. of units	Amount out-standing
1	14	15	16	17	18	19	20	21	22	23	24	25
Assam	–	–	–	–	–	–	–	–	–	–	4	7.30
Meghalaya	–	–	–	–	–	–	1	0.79	–	–	1	0.79
Mizoram	–	–	–	–	–	–	1	0.11	–	–	1	0.11
Bihar	1	2.72	3	3.69	2	2.60	2	9.29	12	23.97	29	56.66
West Bengal	–	–	12	18.47	1	1.77	8	14.77	33	68.60	151	422.38
Orissa	–	–	1	14.66	–	–	3	2.74	2	1.62	9	33.15
Tripura	–	–	–	–	–	–	–	–	1	0.74	1	0.74
Uttar Pradesh	–	–	3	4.56	10	16.90	8	6.63	19	30.12	68	136.37
Delhi	–	–	3	4.09	–	–	–	–	7	22.23	23	51.43
Punjab	–	–	–	–	–	–	2	1.01	5	3.91	21	12.73
Haryana	–	–	4	6.18	–	–	2	0.70	5	4.29	33	50.66

(*Contd*

TABLE 1.3 (*Contd.*)

1	14	15	16	17	18	19	20	21	22	23	24	25
Chandigarh	—	—	—	—	1	0.60	1	0.97	8	6.55	23	40.00
Jammu & Kashmir	—	—	—	—	—	—	—	—	1	1.40	1	1.40
Himachal Pradesh	—	—	—	—	—	—	2	0.41	—	—	5	1.31
Rajasthan	2	24.04	1	1.98	1	0.24	4	3.18	10	6.95	44	80.40
Gujarat	3	1.78	5	14.10	—	—	14	8.20	22	25.24	131	356.57
Maharashtra	1	2.12	16	41.07	5	29.63	27	52.01	55	103.47	252	832.61
Goa	—	—	1	0.22	—	—	1	0.65	10	21.93	15	25.52
Dadra & Nagar Haveli	—	—	—	—	—	—	—	—	1	0.57	1	0.57
Madhya Pradesh	—	—	4	5.53	1	2.79	4	2.14	8	10.09	36	87.59
Andhra Pradesh	—	—	3	3.94	2	6.65	13	22.42	23	34.92	70	119.09
Karnataka	1	5.10	4	13.81	3	20.17	6	3.40	13	8.66	62	127.43
Tamil Nadu	—	—	2	1.83	2	9.02	14	13.13	29	55.02	107	228.90
Kerala	—	—	1	1.07	—	—	5	9.67	12	8.91	27	124.75
Pondicherry	—	—	—	—	—	—	—	—	1	0.74	4	3.33
Total	8	35.76	63	135.20	28	90.37	118	152.22	277	439.93	1119	2801.79

Source: Reserve Bank of India Report on Currency and Finance, 1988-89, pp.72-78.

TABLE 1.4: State-wise and Industry-wise Classification of Non-SSI Sick Industrial Units and Outstanding Bank Credit as at the end of December 1987

(Rupees in crores)

State/Union Territories	Engineering		Electrical		Textiles		Jute		Paper		Rubber	
	No. of units	Amount outstanding	No. of units	Amount outstanding	No. of units	Amount outstanding	No. of units	Amount outstanding	No. of units	Amount outstanding	No. of units	Amount outstanding
1	2	3	4	5	6	7	8	9	10	11	12	13
Assam	—	—	—	—	—	—	—	—	—	—	—	—
Bihar	3	2.98	—	—	1	0.56	2	1.58	—	—	-	—
West Bengal	22	100.33	1	1.10	10	23.65	7	16.18	2	8.19	3	22.61
Orissa	8	5.79	—	—	6	21.21	1	0.69	—	—	—	—
Tripura	—	—	—	—	—	—	1	2.76	—	—	—	—
Uttar Pradesh	6	18.92	—	—	17	108.75	1	1.63	1	1.57	1	2.35
Delhi	1	0.24	—	—	1	3.64	—	—	1	0.41	—	—
Punjab	2	0.90	—	—	2	1.69	—	—	—	—	—	—
Haryana	8	18.22	—	—	2	6.86	—	—	—	—	—	—
Chandigarh	3	3.09	—	—	4	4.77	—	—	1	1.98	—	—
Himachal Pradesh	2	6.36	—	—	3	2.44	—	—	1	0.47	—	—

(Contd.)

TABLE 1.4 (*Contd.*)

1	2	3	4	5	6	7	8	9	10	11	12	13
Rajasthan	2	1.72	1	0.34	7	8.18	—	—	—	—	—	—
Gujarat	8	20.20	2	1.32	28	82.65	—	—	4	2.87	—	—
Maharashtra	35	71.91	2	0.94	43	151.73	—	—	6	9.50	1	4.79
Goa	1	0.07	—	—	—	—	—	—	—	—	—	—
Dadra & Nagar Haveli	—	—	—	—	1	—*	—	—	—	—	—	—
Madhya Pradesh	3	1.92	1	0.24	8	8.36	—	—	—	—	—	—
Andhra Pradesh	13	16.88	1	0.15	6	4.67	2	2.75	3	13.68	—	—
Karnataka	9	28.84	1	1.44	6	14.57	—	—	5	69.50	1	0.26
Tamil Nadu	9	8.55	1	2.65	7	20.05	—	—	1	0.81	—	—
Kerala	6	12.57	2	55.32	5	2.26	—	—	1	11.50	3	4.56
Pondicherry	—	—	—	—	3	11.26	—	—	—	—	—	—
Total	141	319.49	12	63.50	160	477.30	14	25.59	26	120.48	9	34.57

(*Contd.*)

TABLE 1.4 (*Contd.*)

(*Rupees in crores*)

State/Union Territories	Cement		Iron & Steel		Sugar		Chemicals		Miscellaneous		Total	
	No. of units	Amount out-standing	No. of units	Amount out-standing	No. of units	Amount out-standing	No. of units	Amount out-standing	No. of units	Amount out-standing	No. of units	Amount out-standing
1	14	15	16	17	18	19	20	21	22	23	24	25
Assam	—	—	—	—	1	1.31	2	2.08	28	41.71	31	45.10
Bihar	—	—	—	—	2	2.44	—	—	3	8.58	11	16.14
West Bengal	—	—	7	66.02	—	—	9	22.64	58	83.54	119	344.26
Orissa	—	—	2	4.09	—	—	2	0.70	4	4.53	23	37.01
Tripura	—	—	—	—	—	—	—	—	4	0.74	5	3.50
Uttar Pradesh	1	11.50	2	2.01	26	51.22	1	0.81	8	4.77	64	203.53
Delhi	—	—	—	—	—	—	—	—	4	5.45	7	9.74
Punjab	—	—	—	—	—	—	—	—	3	1.34	7	3.93
Haryana	—	—	—	—	—	—	1	0.54	3	2.57	14	28.19
Chandigarh	1	0.43	1	5.19	—	—	2	5.51	2	1.86	14	22.83
Himachal Pradesh	—	—	—	—	—	—	—	—	—	—	6	9.27

(*Contd.*)

TABLE 1.4 (*Contd.*)

1	14	15	16	17	18	19	20	21	22	23	24	25
Rajasthan	1	2.24	—	—	—	—	2	2.12	6	4.92	19	19.52
Gujarat	1	1.46	1	1.47	—	—	4	2.05	10	8.72	58	120.74
Maharashtra	1	25.74	8	10.48	3	0.38	18	18.34	27	63.64	144	357.45
Goa	—	—	—	—	—	—	—	—	7	4.46	8	4.53
Dadra & Nagar Haveli	—	—	—	—	—	—	—	—	—	—	1	—
Madhya Pradesh	—	—	—	—	2	0.62	—	—	3	1.41	17	12.55
Andhra Pradesh	—	—	1	0.29	1	0.24	7	5.66	19	15.11	53	59.43
Karnataka	1	1.86	3	36.97	1	9.40	4	5.50	10	11.48	41	179.82
Tamil Nadu	—	—	1	1.61	2	2.44	4	2.42	20	23.67	45	62.20
Kerala	1	0.75	—	—	—	—	2	3.45	9	14.75	29	105.16
Pondicherry	—	—	—	—	—	—	—	—	1	1.14	4	12.40
Total	7	43.98	26	128.13	38	68.05	58	71.82	229	304.39	720	1657.30

Source: Reserve Bank of India Report on Currency and Finance, 1988-89, pp.79-80.

TABLE 1.5: State-wise Small-Scale Sick Industrial Units and Outstanding Bank Credit as at the end of December 1987

(*Rupees in crores*)

Sl. No.	State/Union Territories	No. of Units	Amount outstanding
1.	Andhra Pradesh	19206	138.48
2.	Assam	9722	19.52
3.	Bihar	14151	73.81
4.	Gujarat	5728	129.91
5.	Goa	673	9.74
6.	Haryana	2096	43.81
7.	Himachal Pradesh	797	8.75
8.	Jammu & Kashmir	2647	11.33
9.	Karnataka	8463	107.72
10.	Kerala	15067	111.18
11.	Madhya Pradesh	12576	55.09
12.	Maharashtra	15401	331.72
13.	Manipur	537	0.66
14.	Meghalaya	120	0.49
15.	Nagaland	16	0.25
16.	Orissa	8692	35.39
17.	Punjab	2434	44.97
18.	Rajasthan	9989	50.50
19.	Tamil Nadu	30942	193.15
20.	Tripura	357	0.56
21.	Uttar Pradesh	19710	148.03
22.	West Bengal	21409	182.43
23.	Andaman Nicobar	—	—
24.	Arunachal Pradesh	11	0.02
25.	Dadra Nagar Haveli	6	0.15
26.	Delhi	3014	92.06
27.	Mizoram	—	—
28.	Pondicherry	271	1.93
29.	Sikkim	4	0.22
30.	Chandigarh	217	5.76
31.	Diu and Daman	3	0.13
	Total	204259	1797.31

Source: RBI Report on Currency and Finance 1988-89, p.81.

Reserve Bank of India, commercial banks and financial institutions have been striving hard and spending a sizeable amount of resources for preventing the spread of industrial sickness and for revival of sick units. The setting up of the Board for Industrial and Financial

Reconstruction (BIFR) under the Sick Industrial Companies (Special Provisions) Act, 1985 is a major step in this direction. The Board became operational in May 1987. The formation of the Board for Industrial and Financial Reconstruction shows the Union Government's apparent seriousness to combat industrial sickness that engulfs the industrial panorama menacingly. However, the preventive measures and revival programmes initiated by the government, financial and non-financial agencies have not made much dent. The increasing trend of sickness both in large and small scale industrial units is no where in control despite policies and actions initiated at various levels. It has become a national problem requiring a comprehensive redress rather than inventing quick fixes to stem industrial sickness and to revive sick units. Hence, a coherent framework consisting of the dynamics of corporate sickness, forewarning system and effective turnaround strategies is required to initiate timely actions to stem the number of sick industrial units multiplying, rehabilitate the viable sick units and decide about the fate of non-viable sick units.

THE CONCEPT OF SICKNESS

Sickness in industries has been viewed from several stand points — economic, legal, managerial and social. Walter (1957) and Donaldson (1962, 1969) had termed it as technical insolvency when a firm is unable to meet its maturing obligations. Others restrict the term to the so-called real insolvency case where the total value of the firm's assets is smaller than its liabilities. Sometimes business failure is interpreted in the strict legal sense of bankruptcy or liquidation when the firm ceases its operations (Altman, 1971). The State Bank of India defines a sick unit 'as one which fails to generate internal surplus on a continuing basis and depends for its survival on frequent infusion of external funds'. Though this definition incorporates the concept of 'cash break even point', it appears to be silent on two crucial questions of 'how much' and for how many years. State Financial Corporations define sickness in terms of defaults in payment of loan instalments. Any unit which has failed to pay three consecutive instalments of interest and/or principal has been classified as sick.

The Industrial Development Bank of India (IDBI) has laid down the following criteria for the identification of sick units:

(a) Continuous cash losses for a period of two years or continued erosion on the net-worth, say 50 per cent;
(b) Continuous default in meeting four consecutive half-yearly instalments of interest or principal of institutional loans;
(c) Shortfall in the margin of bank advances and persisting irregularities in operation of the units credit limit with banks; and
(d) Mounting arrears on account of statutory or other liabilities, say for a period of one or two years.

The Development Commissioner (SSI) followed the following criteria for defining sickness:

(a) Erosion of networth by 50 per cent and more;
(b) Units being closed for a total period of 6 months and more during the last year;
(c) Default in payment of loan instalments;
(d) Capacity utilisation less than 50 per cent of the highest achieved during the preceding 5 years.

i ,eping the above in view, there can be at least three different view-points in defining sickness:

(a) At the government level in India, corporate sickness gets recognised generally only when a unit is on the brink of closure or closes its doors, throwing a large number of people out of employment;
(b) At the institutional level, the problem gets recognised when non-payment of instalments due to money lent starts and continues for two or three intervals i.e. recovery of money lent becomes uncertain;
(c) From the shareholders point of view, an enterprise is considered sick if it fails to pay reasonable dividends and its future also looks bleak and the share value tumbles down.

A review of three different view-points defining sickness brings to bear that the third view is nearer the economic sense of the term failure. It is related to the earning potential of the enterprise and the second view is nearer to the business sense of the term failure.

To clarify certain ambiguities regarding the term sickness and to evolve a single definition of a sick unit acceptable to all concerned, Sick Industrial Companies (Special Provisions) Act (SICA), 1985 and Reserve Bank of India have defined a sick industrial unit in Indian context as under:

Non-SSI Sick Unit (Covered by SICA, 1985)

According to the Sick Industrial Companies (Special Provisions) Act, 1985, 'sick industrial company' means a medium and large (i.e. non-SSI) industrial company (being a company registered for not less than 7 years) which has at the end of any financial years accumulated losses equal to or exceeding its entire net worth and has also suffered cash losses in such financial year and the financial year immediately preceding such financial year. This definition does not cover, government companies, shipping companies and small-scale industrial units/ancillary units. Further, an industrial unit will be termed as 'weak' if at the end of any accounting year it has: (i) accumulated losses equal to or exceeding 50 per cent of its peak net-worth in the immediately preceding five accounting years; (ii) a current ratio of less than 1: 1; and (iii) suffered a cash loss in the immediately preceding accounting year.

Non-SSI Weak Unit (Not covered by SICA, 1985)

With a view to cover the categories of industrial units (non-SSI sick units), which do not come under the purview of the Sick Industrial Companies (Special Provisions) Act, 1985, the RBI has advised the banks to take the necessary remedial measures in respect of industrial units at the stage of 50 per cent erosion of their net worth. Such units, have been termed as 'weak' units to distinguish them from 'sick industrial companies' as defined in the Act. An industrial undertaking is termed 'weak' if at the end of any accounting year, it has: (i) accumulated losses equal to or exceeding 50 per cent of its peak networth in the immediately preceding five accounting years, (ii) a current ratio of less than 1:1, and (iii) suffered a cash loss in the immediately preceding accounting year.

SSI Sick Unit

A SSI unit should be considered 'sick' if it has: (a) incurred cash loss in the previous accounting year and is likely to continue to incur cash loss in the current accounting year and has an erosion on account of cumulative cash losses to the extent of 50 per cent or more of its net worth and/or (b) continuously defaulted in meeting four consecutive quarterly instalments of interest or two half-yearly instalments of principal on term loans and there are persistent irregularities in the operation of its credit limits with the bank. While both the conditions (a) and (b) should be satisfied in the case of larger SSI units, it would suffice if either alternative (a) or (b) is satisfied in case of the tiny and decentralised sector units. However, in the case of such units if it is difficult to get financial particulars, a unit may be considered as "Sick" if it defaults continuously for a period of one year, in the payment of interest or instalment of principal and there are persistent irregularities in the operation of the credit limit with the banks.

Presently the above definitions of sickness are being followed by all concerned in India to identify sick units in large, medium and small scale industries.

The Bureau of Public Enterprises (BPE) has defined a sick public sector unit as the one which has eroded 100 per cent of its equity and has been incurring losses continuously for the last five years. The BPE has also suggested the criterion for identifying the potential units which should be assisted to improve their health. The sick units are divided into four categories: (a) those loss-making units which bear high social costs and face low competition, (b) units facing high social costs and high competition, (c) units bearing a low social costs and low competition (d) units bearing low social burden and high competition. The BPE has suggested that the matter of public sector sick units should also be referred to the Board for Industrial and Financial Reconstruction (BIFR) which has been incorporated in the Central Government Budget, 1991-92. Fifty public sector undertakings which have been making losses continuously for the last five years, have been identified and will be referred to the Board for Industrial and Financial Reconstruction for proper course of action (*The Hindustan Times*, October 26, 1991).

WHY DO RUNNING UNITS FALL SICK?

Substantial empirical work has been carried out on the causes of growing phenomenon of industrial sickness and diverse views have been expressed (Argenti 1976; Ross and Kami, 1973; Kharbanda and

Stallworthy, 1987; Altman 1983; Allsop, 1977; Khandwalla 1988). A large number of factors both external and internal operating in combination or singly are responsible for the decline of a unit. A unit could become sick due to one or combination of the various factors. These include poor management, inadequate information and reporting system, poor implementation, poor market survey, lack of market penetration, poor product mix strategy, seasonal demand for products, recession, inefficient operation of plant and machinery, poor maintenance and replacement of components, obsolete technology, under-utilisation of capacity, shortage of power, lack of proper production planning and control, high material wastage, labour unrest, deliberate diversion of funds, poor management of working capital, poor capital structure, overtrading, environmental factors etc. One of the basic causes of growing sickness on which there is a fairly wide consensus is the poor management. Smith (1966) found that the basic reasons for company failures are: autocratic management, resistance to change, lack of control, over-diversification, bad luck and too much decentralisation. Ross and Kami (1973) indicated that it is the bad management which is to be blamed for corporate failures and suggested a list of 'ten commandments' of effective management. Bad management is to break one or more of them resulting in Corporate Crisis. These are:

1. Management must have a strategy and communicate it.
2. There must be overall controls and cost controls.
3. The board must actively participate.
4. Avoid one-man rule.
5. Provide management depth.
6. Keep informed and react to change.
7. The customer is king.
8. Do not misuse computers.
9. Do not engage in accounting manipulations.
10. Provide an organised structure that knows people's needs.

Argenti (1967, p.123) in his book *Corporate Collapse: The Causes and Symptoms* pointed out that the prime cause of failure is bad management. Good managers will seldom make the same fatal mistakes as poor managers, but if they do make them, their managerial ability will protect the company from the worst consequences. He described six top management structural defects by which a bad management can be identified: one-man rule, non-participating board, unbalanced top team, lack of management depth, weak finance function and combined chairman-chief executive. Slatter (1984) in his book *Corporate Recovery* identified twelve causes of decline:

- Lack of financial control,
- Inadequate management,
- Price and product competition,
- High cost structure,
- Changes in market demands,
- Adverse movements in commodity markets,
- Lack of marketing effort,
- Big projects,
- Acquisitions,
- Poor financial policy,
- Over trading, and
- Organisational structure.

He further pointed out that it is rare that any one factor by itself will precipitate the need for recovery action. The need for recovery is usually brought about by a combination of factors, although lack of financial control and poor management stand out as the most frequent causes.

Bibeault (1982) based on a study of American companies, found that internal causes of decline such as one-man rule, lack of management depth, management change problem, inbred bureaucratic management, weak finance function, an unbalanced top management team and finally a weak and non-participative board accounted for about 70 per cent of corporate declines. In another 20 per cent of the cases, internal reasons were partially responsible for decline. External factors such as exchange rate changes, credit squeezes, slumps, inflation etc. were responsible for the remaining 10 per cent of the corporate declines. In Indian context, a study of 378 large sick units commissioned by the Reserve Bank of India in 1981 also indicated that about two-thirds of the units had become sick due to mismanagement of one kind or another — diversion of funds, infighting, lack of marketing strategies, faulty project planning and faulty choice of technology (Morris, 1982, p. 47). Other causes identified by the RBI study are market recession (23 per cent) and labour problems, raw material shortage, power shortage etc. (11 per cent). In an analysis of 223 sick industrial projects, poor management has been identified as the most significant factor which contributes over 43 per cent to the sickness in industry (Srivastava and Yadav, 1986). The number of sick industrial units, percentage of the units and percentage contribution of each cause is shown in Table 1.6. On further analysis, it is observed that lack of proper information and reporting system, especially accounting information, is the significant factor associated with poor management that contribute to sickness. The several deficiencies noticed concerning the information and reporting system are: (i) no or poor cash flow planning, (ii) no or poor costing system, (iii) no or poor budgetary system, and (iv) the poor reporting of faults, break downs and sales. The lack of adequate information and reporting system decreases the ability of the management seeing the approaching disaster, with the result corrective measures are not taken in time. It results in management's inability to respond to changes, which then becomes a major cause of sickness. These factors, if not controlled, start creating conditions which force a unit to turn from a healthy state to one tending towards sickness and then through incipient sickness to a gravely sick stage. Each sick unit starts throwing up signals and symptoms (Fig. 1.1) in operational areas of management which need to be identified and monitored before the unit becomes gravely sick.

TABLE 1.6: Cause-wise Distribution of Sick Industrial Units

Causes of sickness	No. of sick units	% of sick units	% contribution of the cause to sickness
Lack of good management	36	16.1	22.19
Poor implementation	56	25.1	21.70
Marketing problems	29	13.1	15.81
Non-availability of raw materials	53	23.8	13.45
Shortage of working capital	03	01.4	07.20
Labour trouble	12	05.4	05.74
Technical operational problems	13	05.8	05.55
Other causes	21	09.4	08.36

However, a mere list of causes of sickness, no matter how comprehensive it my be, is not enough unless linked together in a mechanism leading to sickness. Hence, the dynamics of sickness — the sequencing of events that bind together all the causes and symptoms of sickness in industrial units is illustrated in Fig. 1.2.

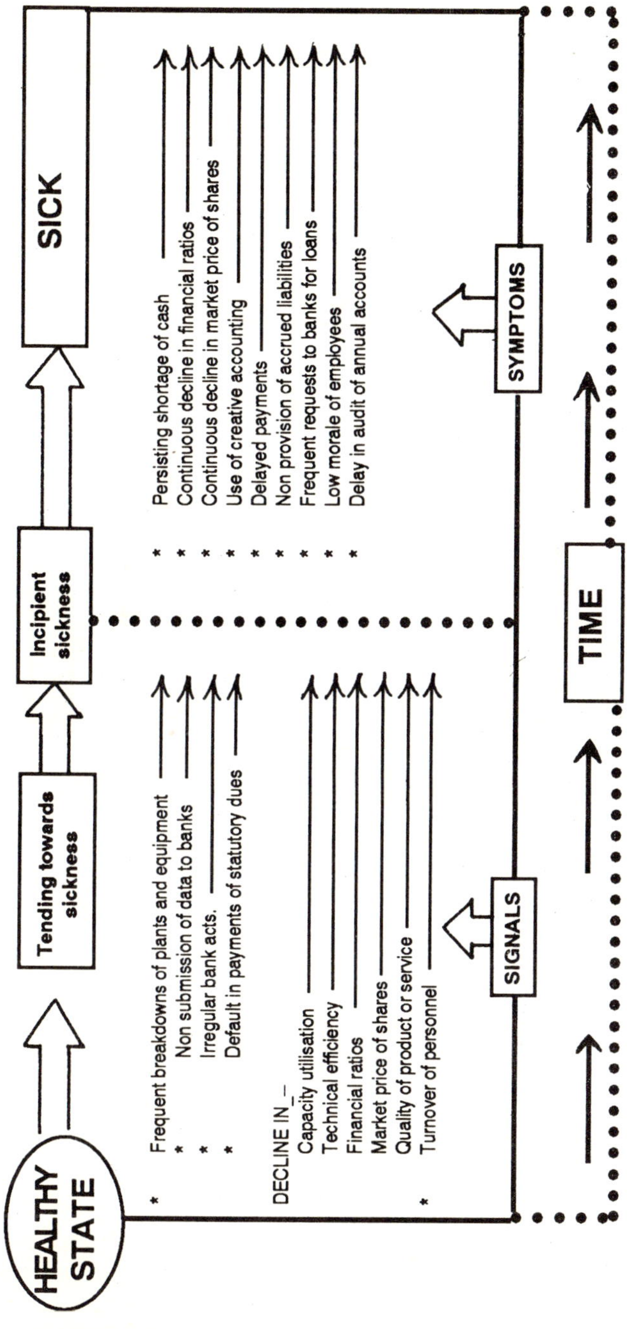

FIG. 1.1: Signals and Symptoms of Sickness

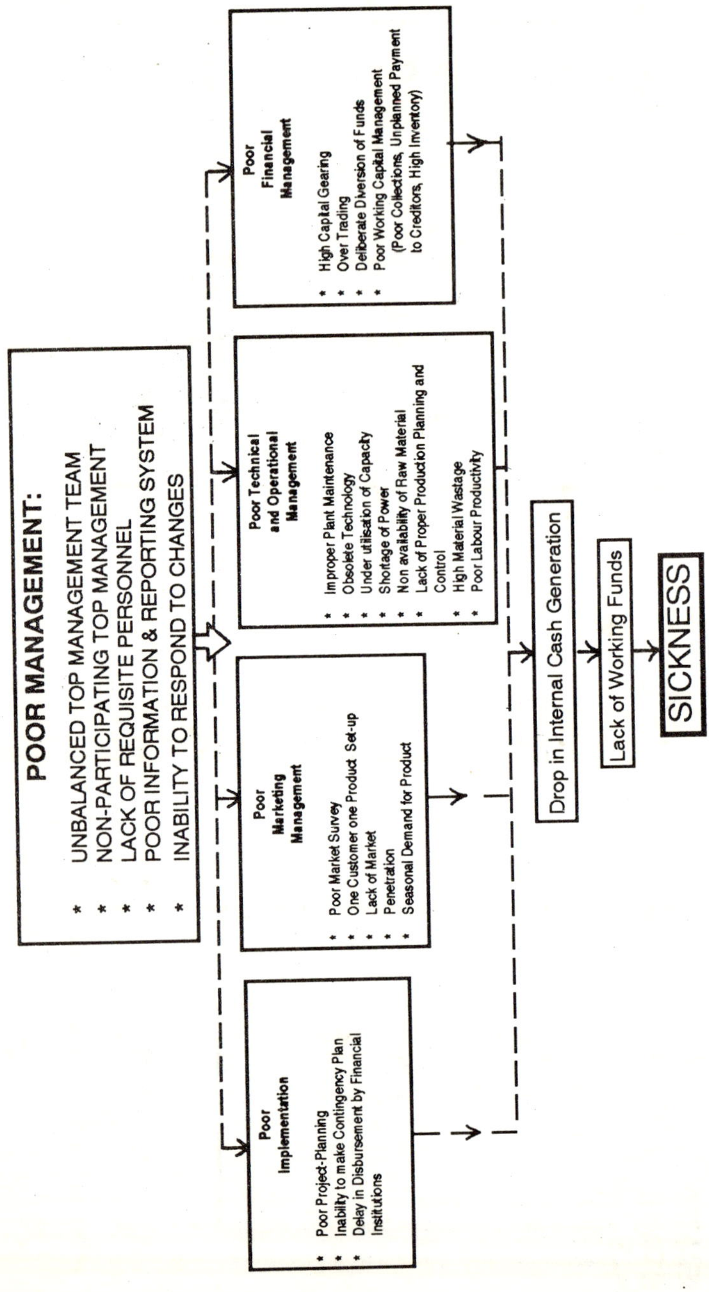

FIG. 4.2: Internal Factors Causing Industrial Sickness

Categorisation of Sick Units

Having studied and analysed the industrial units falling in the sick category, sick industrial units may be grouped in three areas:

(a) Born Sick,
(b) Made Sick,
(c) Sickness is thrust on them.

Poor appraisal, second-hand plant and equipment, inadequate market survey, poor implementation, one customer-one product type situation result into born sick units. Poor management, diversion of funds etc. contribute to the second category of sick industrial units, Changes in government policies, strategic shortage of raw materials, sudden withdrawal of government subsidies due to political reasons etc., lead to sickness in industries which is beyond their control and can be attributed to environmental factors. Hence, appropriate preventive and remedial actions will depend on the diagnosis of causes of sickness in industrial units falling under the above categories and identification of the critical parameters responsible for it.

SICKNESS IS AN ORGANIC PROCESS

Sickness in an industry is an organic process in the life history of units. A healthy unit may become sick temporarily and may recover or *vice versa*. Factors that cause sickness could be internal or external. The external factors usually affect all the industrial units in the same group while the internal factors may affect a particular unit only and not the whole industry. In such cases, the sickness has an origin followed by several stages of sickness. The sickness process is illustrated in Fig. 1.3. Initially a healthy unit shows good cash profit and may have positive values of net working capital and net worth. As it tends towards sickness, the first (cash profit) may become negative although the unit may continue to pay its instalments to the term lending institutions. As sickness grows more and more through other stages, two or more financial parameters may become negative. The negative values do signal sickness. It is these initial stages that require careful monitoring. For such a purpose, a forewarning system which signals the probable sickness of industrial concerns before any loss is inflicted upon the concerned parties would prove to be a great boon. It would provide a warning to all the concerned parties to reconsider their situation and take prompt and appropriate action.

It is a well established fact that earlier the trouble is detected, more easily and economically it may be countered. Early detection of sickness possibly may enable the management to take timely action to avert the crisis of such an occurrence. If there exists a forewarning system which helps in predicting corporate sickness, the attention can be focussed on those concerns which are trudging towards sickness. Companies do not go burst 'overnight' as many people think. The process of sickness can take years and thus the seeds of sickness may be discernible very early in the story of a company's rise and decline. The forewarning system would help in reducing, if not completely eliminating, the irreparable loss to the interested parties caused by corporate collapse. The importance of such a forewarning system can be described in the words of Lev (p. 134) more clearly: 'An early warning signal of probable failure will enable both management and investors to take preventive measures; operating policy changes, reorganisation of financial structure, and even voluntary liquidation will usually shorten the length of time losses are incurred and thereby improve both private and social resource allocation'.

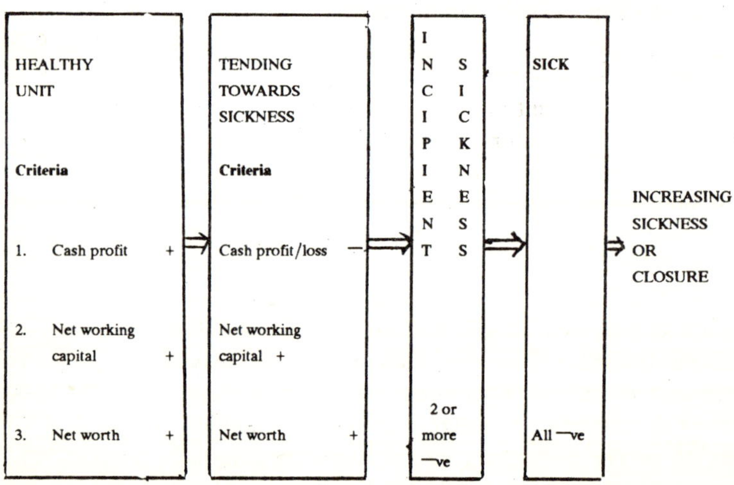

FIG. 1.3: The Sickness Process

In our set-up today, owners' stake in most of our industries is limited. A substantial risk of the venture many a times is taken by the commercial banks and financial institutions apart from the equity holders. This puts an additional responsibility on the banks and financial institutions to ensure an effective utilisation of credit and to prevent misutilisation by the borrowers. The rationale for prediction of sickness in advance of its occurrence is to save crores of rupees of banks, financial institutions and other investors for better use which otherwise would be locked up in sick units with little chance of recovery. It thus, becomes necessary that sickness in units should be predicted and closely monitored to safeguard the interest of all concerned.

WHEN TO DIAGNOSE AND TREAT?

The objective of the Sick Industrial Companies Legislation, 1985 is to enable early detection of sickness in an industrial unit and to evolve a package of measures to remove uncertainty about the working of the sick unit. The legislation is intended to securing timely detection of sick and potential sick units, the speedy detection by a body of experts of the preventive, ameliorative, remedial and other measures which need to be taken with respect to such companies and expeditious enforcement of these measures.

For the purpose of detecting sickness in an industrial unit at an incipient stage and then to evolve a package of measures to remove the uncertainties about the working of the sick unit, the sickness of the unit has been appraised at two levels:

(i) When the erosion of the net worth is of the order of 50 per cent, the Board of Directors of the sick unit has been asked to bring this fact to the notice of the shareholders within a period of 60 days from the date of finalisation of the detailed audited accounts of the company for the relevant financial year.

(ii) When the erosion of the net worth is 100 per cent and more and the unit continues to show cash losses for the next two years, the management of unit is required to report to the newly constituted Board under the Legislation which would then take appropriate actions which may involve merging, rehabilitation or even winding up after a fresh appraisal through an operating agency.

A unit likely to be sick starts showing cash losses in the initial years, leading to the loss of working capital which it tries to manipulate by borrowings. The erosion of net worth is a slow process. It may take several years of sickness before 50 per cent erosion of net worth takes place and it is likely that from the appearance of first signal and symptoms of sickness to 100 per cent erosion of net worth, it may be six to ten years of continuing sickness. Analysis of some of the sick units is given in Table 1.7 to support this fact.

The financial data of 11 sick industrial units randomly selected have been analysed and presented in Table 1.7 where the time gap between first appearance of sickness and 100 per cent erosion of net worth is shown. The first appearance of sickness is measured in terms of negative working capital and cash losses, though there are other financial and non-financial parameters also to measure it. The analysis of the data in Table 1.7 shows that the working capital becomes negative to start with followed by cash losses. The 50 per cent erosion of net worth takes seven to eight years. This period is quite crucial. At this stage, the unit enters into a state of grave sickness, because the landslide from 50 per cent erosion to 100 per cent erosion in less than two years. A sick unit at 50 per cent erosion of net worth is thus in a grave state of sickness. And thus the actions recommended at 50 per cent erosion of net worth would then merge with what is required at 100 per cent erosion of net worth as there would hardly be much time to do any thing by the share-holders and the Board of the unit.

The mode of early detection of sickness as outlined in the legislation is thus not adequate and hence, will not meet its objectives. In fact, according to the standards laid down, a unit would be considered sick at a level of 50 per cent erosion of its net worth and gravely sick (in fact nearing collapsing) at 100 per cent erosion of its net worth. Thus the objective of the legislation in respect of early detection of sickness is not met.

The early detection of sickness can be made through a process of monitoring the financial status of the company in respect of working capital, cash losses and erosion of net worth. Each sick unit starts giving rise to signals and symptoms in these and other areas of management which need to be taken note of.

The definition of sickness, i.e. at 50 per cent erosion of peak net worth, helps to identify only too late a stage for action to prevent industrial sickness. As already mentioned, this is really a grave state of sickness and not an early stage of sickness. It is, therefore, necessary to redefine the state of sickness of a unit.

TABLE 1.7: Time Gap between First Appearance of Sickness and 100 Per Cent Erosion of Net Worth

Name of Companies	Year of negative working capital	Year of cash loss	Year of 50% erosion of net worth	Year of 100% erosion of net worth
1. Mysore Spg. & Co Ltd.	1964	1965	1971	1972
2. The Elphinstone Spg. & Wvg. Mills Ltd.	1963	1967	1975	1976
3. The Ahmedabad Jupiter Spg. Wvg. & Mfg. Co. Ltd.	1963	1967	1970	1971
4. The Aurangabad Mills Ltd.	1963	1962	1970	1971
5. The Azamjahi Mills Ltd.	1962	1963	1968	1969
6. The Himabai Mfg. Co Ltd.	1962	1965	1967	1968
7. The Jehangir Vikil Mills Co. Ltd.	1961	1966	1969	1970
8. The Tata Mills Ltd.	1963	1968	1977	1980
9. The Indore Malwa United Mills Ltd.	1963	1965	1968	1969
10. The Cannanore Spg. & Wvg. Mills Ltd.	1964	1966	1969	1971
11. India Paper Pulp Co. Ltd.	1968	1967	1970	1973

Sickness in the early stages can be identified through a monitoring process of the working capital, cash losses and erosion of net worth up to 15 per cent (Fig. 1.4). This state of affairs lasts for two to three years. There are ample signals and symptoms, both financial and non-financial, (as shown in Fig. 1.1) available in this period of sickness which should be adequate for the management to take necessary action. The action which is recommended at 50 per cent erosion of net worth should really be taken when the net worth erosion is 15 per cent and not more. Such a definition of sickness would then put pressure on the management of companies to look to their operational performance and to evolve a management information system which should enable them to detect the onset of sickness at an early stage which is the objective of the legislation. Hence, there should be an emphasis on having a management information reporting system within every company and the Board of

Directors should be given a mandate to report the incipient sickness when a unit starts showing cash losses and negative working capital and take appropriate measures when net worth starts eroding 10 to 15 per cent.

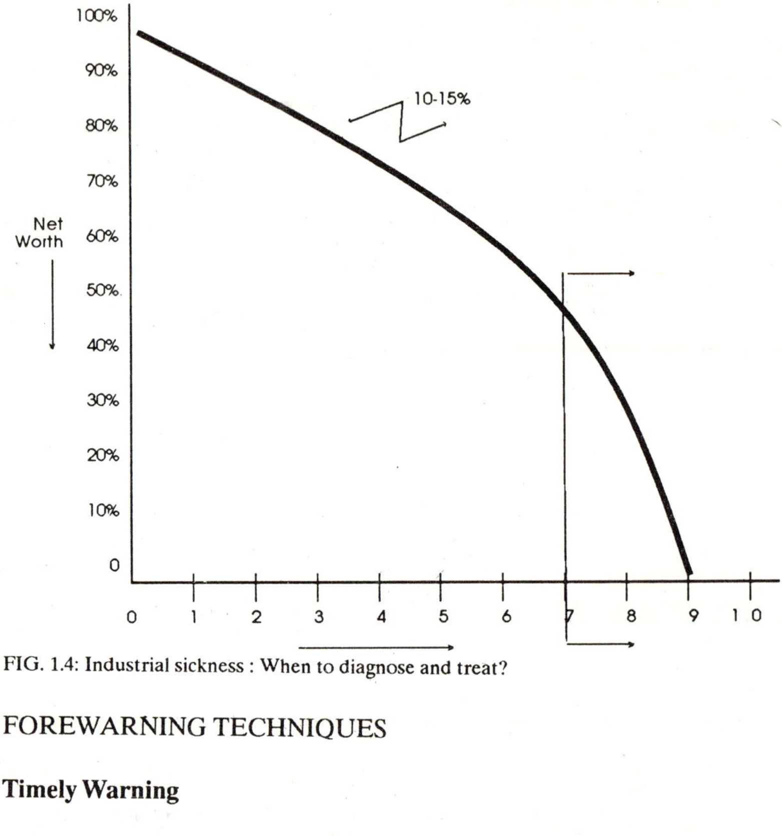

FIG. 1.4: Industrial sickness : When to diagnose and treat?

FOREWARNING TECHNIQUES

Timely Warning

Sick units start throwing up a large number of signals and symptoms (Fig. 1.1) which can be identified before they become gravely sick. An industrial unit tends to show the signs of financial distress starting with short-term liquidity problems, operating losses and moving in the direction of overuse of external credit until it reaches a stage where it is overburdened with debt and not able to muster sufficient funds to meet its obligations. The signals gradually merge into symptoms and get related to plant performance, capacity utilisation, financial ratios, share market price, use of creative accounting, quality of product or service and labour relations. The early detection of sickness can be made by monitoring the financial parameters of a unit in respect of working capital, cash losses and erosion of net worth. Sickness is an organic process in the life history of a unit. A healthy unit may become sick temporarily and recover or *vice versa*. The sickness process is illustrated in Fig. 1.3. Initially a healthy unit may show good profit and may have positive values of net working capital and net worth. As it tends towards sickness, one of these may become negative, although the unit may continue to pay its instalments to the lending institutions. As sickness grows, more and more financial parameters may become negative. The negative values do signal sickness.

The existence of these signals and symptoms is a good ground for suspecting that the industrial unit concerned is prone to sickness, but the magnitude of sickness cannot be predicted on these alone. Hence, an objective analysis is to be made to predict the on-set of sickness in industrial units.

Univariate and Multivariate Analysis

Some empirical work has been carried out in India and abroad and various techniques have been developed to predict the on-set of sickness in industrial units. But the manner in which various parameters are presently being applied to appraise industrial health is not very reliable and accurate. There is considerable vagueness and misunderstanding as to which parameters are significant and what values are really critical to detect industrial sickness. Keeping the above in view, an attempt has been made to develop a more scientific quantitative multivariate approach to predict industrial sickness (Yadav, 1986).

The study is based on the initial sample of 78 industrial units consisting of 39 sick and 39 non-sick units. The sample was taken on the basis of paired sample design. The paired sample design was chosen to reduce and control over the impact of other variables such as industry, size, age and fiscal year that otherwise might have blurred the relationship between financial ratios and sickness. The matching of the units was made in terms of industry, size, age and fiscal year. The units included in the study are stratified over 11 industrial groups and limited to manufacturing concerns only. The study is based on the financial statement prepared under the currently accepted reporting standards and examination of the predictive power of 36 financial ratios univariately as well as multivariately by using various statistical techniques such as *t*-test, dichotomous classification test, factor analysis, *F*-test and discriminant analysis.

Univariate Approach

The results drawn on the basis of univariate techniques known as *t*-test and dichotomous classification test have shown that the financial ratios taken individually can predict sickness. But there is relative difference in the predictive power of financial ratios. The cash flow to total tangible assets ratio (CF/TTA) has been found possessing the highest predictive power followed by the earning before interest and taxes to total tangible assets (EBIT/TTA) ratio. Among the solvency and liquidity ratios, solvency ratios are found to be more reliable predictors of industrial health than liquidity ratios. The empirical results indicate that the units with heavy debt and inadequate equity base are more prone to sickness. All liquidity ratios proved to be vary poor in predicting industrial health. The current ratio and quick ratio have resulted three and a half times more classification error than the best profitability ratio. It contradicts the considerable importance traditionally attached to liquidity ratios in appraising health of an industrial unit. The net cash flow from operations to the reservoir has been found the most critical factor, while the size of the reservoir is the least important factor in detecting industrial sickness.

It should, however, be noted that the univariate approach is a crude technique of predicting industrial sickness because each ratio is considered individually and thus indicates only the individual information value of a ratio. It ignores the interdependencies among the various ratios (Horrigan, 1965; Lev, 1969). It may result in ambiguous inferences on account of conflicting signals. For instance, a firm with poor profitability ratio may be classified as a potential sick unit, but, however, the situation may not be considered serious on account of its above average liquidity ratio. Keeping in view the limitations of univariate analysis, an attempt has been made to overcome its shortcomings by the use of multivariate analysis in which several ratios are combined into a model to predict industrial sickness.

Multivariate Discriminant Analysis – (MDA) Model

From the original list of 36 financial ratios, four variables have been found the sensitive ones which contribute most towards the prediction of industrial sickness. A multi-ratio model containing four financial ratios serving as the best predictive variables of industrial sickness has been developed by using various statistical techniques known as F-test, factor analysis and discriminant analysis. The best discriminant function investigated is as under (Yadav, 1986, p. 88):

$$Y = 19.8927\,V_1 + 0.0047\,V_2 + 0.7141\,V_3 + 0.4860\,V_4$$

Where

Y = Overall discriminant score;

V_1 = Earning before interest and taxes (EBIT)[1] to total tangible assets (TTA);

V_2 = Current assets (CA) to current liabilities (CL);

V_3 = Net sales (NS) to total tangible assets (TTA);

V_4 = Defensive assets (DA) to total operating expenditures (TOE). (This ratio is known as 'Defensive Interval Ratio').

The discriminant model so developed is not claimed to be optimal since the process is iterative. It, however, does the best job among the alternatives which involve numerous computer runs and analysis of various financial ratio profiles. The multivariate F-ratio is also worked out to test the statistical significance of overall predictive power of the discriminant function. The F-ratio is significant at one per cent level of significance i.e. F = 24.4976 $F_{1,76}$ (0.01) = 6.98 and hence there is no doubt about the overall predictive power of the discriminant function.

The set of variables in the above discriminant function are independent and least correlated with each other in both the groups, namely, sick and non-sick and thus each variable provides additional information about the health of an industrial unit. The contribution of each variable is additional towards the predictive power of the discriminant model. The correlation matrix given in Table 1.8

---

1. In certain cases, it has been observed that non-operating income/loss constitutes a major portion of EBIT. Hence, it is excluded while computing EBIT in such type of cases.

indicates the inter-correlation between the variables in the discriminant model.

TABLE 1.8: Correlation Matrix of Variables in MDA Model

Variables	V_1 EBIT/TTA	V_2 CA/CL	V_3 NS/TTA	V_4 DA/TOE
EBIT/TTA—V_1	1.00	0.189 (0.174)	0.208 (0.391)	0.095 (0.165)
CA/CL—V_2	0.189 (0.174)	1.00	0.176 (0.443)	0.016 (0.196)
NS/TTA—V_3	0.208 (0.391)	0.176 (0.443)	1.00	0.254 (0.421)
DA/TOE—V_4	0.095 (0.165)	0.016 (0.196)	0.254 (0.421)	1.00

Note: Figures in parentheses represent the inter-correlations between variables of non-sick industrial units.

Decision Rule

The discriminant score $Y_c = 1.425$ has been determined as the optimal value to classify the firms either into potentially sick group or non-sick group. If the individual discriminant score of any industrial unit is below $Y_c = 1.425$, it is to be classified as a potentially sick unit and *vice versa*.

The probability of misclassification of the model is also ascertained in order to judge the reliability of accuracy of the model more rigorously. The probability of misclassification of the model is $P_1 = 0.1131$ and $P_2 = 0.1292$ for sick and non-sick units, respectively.

The term 'misclassification' in this context means that assignment of firms to sick or non-sick group on the basis of the model is expected to disagree with the actual or prior classification in 11.31 per cent and 12.92 per cent cases in sick and non-sick group of units, respectively. It means that further examination may be required only in 11.31 per cent units in sick group and 12.92 per cent units in non-sick group in order to classify them correctly. The area falling between 1.33 to 1.52 discriminant series is defined as the 'zone of ignorance or area of uncertainty' because of susceptibility to 'misclassification'. Since errors have been observed in this range of values, there will be uncertainty about a new firm whose *Y*-score value falls within the 'zone of ignorance'. Hence the probability of misclassification of each firm under study falling within the 'zone of ignorance' should be ascertained and used as an additional aid along with the discriminant scores in predicting their chances of falling sick or survival.

Ranking of Variables

The relative contribution of each variable to the total predictive power of the model is determined on the basis of scaled vector or each variable which is computed by multiplying corresponding elements by the square roots of the diagonal elements of the variance-co-variance matrix. Since the actual variable measurements of units are not comparable to each other, simple observation of the discriminant coefficients may mislead. The adjusted coefficients (i.e. scaled vector) therefore, are computed and presented in Table 1.9.

TABLE 1.9: Scaled Vector Indicating Relative Contribution of Variables

Variable	Sealed vector	Ranking
EBIT/TTA	2.009	1
CA/CL	0.033	4
NS/TTA	0.885	2
DA/TOE	0.298	3

The scaled vectors presented in Table 1.9 clearly indicate that profitability ratio (EBIT/TTA) contributes the most followed by turnover ratio (NS/TTA) towards the predictive power of the model.

Predictive Accuracy of the Model

Initial Sample: The predictive power of the model has been examined over a period of six years prior to the date of sickness for the initial sample and summarised in Table 1.10 which clearly indicates that the model is accurate in predicting industrial sickness though with decreasing probability. The fall in the predictive accuracy of the model is logically understandable taking into account the long period that elapses, because the indications of the ratios become less and less clear as the lead time from the date of sickness increases.

TABLE 1.10: Predictive Accuracy of the Model

Year prior to sickness	Number of units	Number correctly classified	Number misclassified	% of correct classification
1	78	74	04	95
2	78	68	10	87
3	76	65	11	86
4	72	59	13	82
5	63	50	13	79
6	51	40	11	78

Test Samples: The model is applied to a series of additional samples of sick and non-sick industrial units taken both from homogeneous and non-homogeneous groups of industries to judge its validity and effectiveness. These samples are taken at random irrespective of size, fiscal year and age of units. The importance of test samples cannot be overemphasised since the real efficiency of the model lies in predicting the sickness for a unit which is not used to develop the parameters of the model. The model has been successfully used to predict sickness in nine industrial groups comprising over 20 units in each. The nine industrial groups studied are textile, jute, paper, chemical and pharmaceutical, iron and steel, electrical, engineering, sugar and rubber. The predictive accuracy of the model is summarised in Table 1.11.

TABLE 1.11: Percentage Classification Error in Predicting Sickness

Year prior to sickness	In non-homogeneous group		In homogeneous group
	Initial sample	Test sample	Test samples of sick textile units
1	05	04.17	00.01
2	13	04.17	02.78
3	14	09.52	02.86
4	18	06.25	06.06
5	21	13.33	09.09
6	22	13.33	12.91

Empirical results indicate that the predictive accuracy of the model is very high in homogeneous and non-homogeneous groups of industrial units, though the overall performance of the model in case of homogeneous group is better compared to that of non-homogeneous group. It may be due to the homogeneity of the industry group to which the model is applied.

2

TURNAROUND
Stages and Strategies

THE CONCEPT

The word "turnaround" has been gaining significance in the world of business in the context of increasing phenomenon of business failure. Turnaround means a substantial and sustainable positive change in the performance of a unit through determined efforts. To put it in simple words, it implies producing a noticeable and durable improvement in performance from down to up, from not good enough to better, from unsatisfactory performance to acceptable and from losing to achieving. It is an attempt to revitalise an enterprise whose performance both in financial and non-financial terms is below the level projected or which stands out of line with the general run of the business in the same industry group. Experts describe turnaround as sustainable recovery of a sick unit leading to its normal growth and profitability. In a study of 54 American companies (Schendel, Patton and Riggs, 1976, p.3) turnaround is defined as a decline and recovery in performance. It refers to a four-years of increase in income relative to Gross National Product (GNP), following a four years of decline in income relative to GNP with a two-years stabilisation period between the downturn and upturn phases. Hambrick and Schecter (1983) in their study based on 260 companies puts turnaround as an average return on investment of at least 20 per cent for two years following a two-years period in which the average return was less than 10 per cent. Bibeault (1982, p.125) explains it, "a company has not really turned around unless it has achieved a solid basis of future growth". Slatter (1984, p.15) defines turnaround as sustainable recovery of a sick firm. He explains, "Sustainable recovery involves achieving a viable and desirable business strategy, supported by an adequate organisation and control structure". An Indian expert explains, "A full turnaround would be a situation where the profitability has approached industry levels and has stabilised at least at these levels" (Khandwalla, 1989, p.47). The sustainable recovery of a sick firm may be measured in terms of its net worth, net working capital, cash profit to total tangible assets and health score. The comparison in terms of the above parameters with the past performance of the firm and with the industry levels would indicate the extent of its sickness and recovery.

The turnaround opportunities should be recognised as inevitable because of changing scenario of business world on account of some fundamental reasons such as rapid changes in the technological and economic areas together, complexity of socio-political processes etc. Business units always have problems but these vary in magnitude and complexity. Most of the companies in their life-cycle are likely to face a turnaround situation, whether they recover, continue to stagnate or go into liquidation depends on their management and its turnaround strategies. For successful turnaround, the company should be a viable unit and should have management that is sensitive to internal as well as external challenges. Successful turnaround performance calls for in-depth management knowledge, penetrating ability, ruthless adherence to objectives, a great deal of self-confidence, hard work and human energy of a high order.

A turnaround situation is an extraordinary period in the life history of a company. It requires unique and substantially different management approaches compared to normal situation. An Indian study (Khandwall, 1989, p.122) based on ten cases consisting three of successful turnarounds, three of unsuccessful ones and four of partially successful turnarounds indicates that the turnaround management differs in several ways from the professional management of healthy units: (i) change of existing top management is nearly an essential requirement in a turnaround, but in case of healthy unit it may prove disruptive, (ii) there is heavy involvement of the top management both in strategic and operating management especially during initial stages in a turnaround, (iii) the top management performs a much wider range of activities during turnaround compared to normal times such as asset liquidation, cost reduction, revenue generation, negotiating with stakeholders, mobilising the organisation, coordination etc. The chief executive has to bear the brunt of these multi-faceted activities, (iv) during turnaround, the emphasis of top management is to identifying quick pay off projects, credibility building, getting ready the staff for extraordinary efforts, negotiating with the owners, funding institutions and government for temporary relief and support for the turnaround effort, and (v) 'the name of the game in a turnaround is improvisation, crisis management, mobilisation, selective plugging of the largest loopholes in the system, out-and out-opportunism in seizing anything profitable, and short-term expediency. In contrast, long term considerations, professional modes of functioning, principled stands, emphasis on proper systems etc. characterise normal functioning'. Many of the effective management tenets as applied in the cases of normal situations lose their validity in case of turnaround situation. In most cases, turnaround follows several years of declining profitability which usually culminates in substantial losses threatening the financial viability of the unit. However, declining performance may not always threaten the financial viability of the unit, but it has serious negative impact on the health and when the performance of a company either as a whole or in one of its departments is consistently found below the average in its industry group, it calls for special efforts to raise performance above the group average, and thus becomes a turnaround situation.

The time span of a turnaround begins with the recognition of the need and the opportunities and continues with the development of a total programme of action which leads to the achievement of consistent improvement in performance and return to normal growth. This kind of reconstruction generally cannot be achieved overnight, since the causes of prolonged sickness in a company are deep rooted. To overcome these and to build a new winning way of corporate life requires considerable time. However, the noteworthy thing is the 'Timing' for turnaround since the unit is bleeding in the form of losses of millions of rupees daily. A typical profile of a major turnaround is described as one to three years to bottom out, then two years of improved earnings taking the company towards its desired level of performance (Goodman, 1982, p.13). In an American study based on 81 companies, Bibeault (1982, p.3) describes that 'the average duration of the upturn recovery was 4.1 years with larger companies taking longer to turnaround and smaller taking less time'. The above profile of turnaround period has been observed in most of the Indian cases too, though there have been some cases of spectacular recovery taking as short period as one year. Damodar Valley Corporation (DVC) turnaround is a good example where

Mr. Luther increased the plant load factor by 54 per cent within a year.

TURNAROUND STRATEGY

Strategy is a comprehensive and integrated blue-print or plan designed for getting the organisation where it wants to go. It refers to the determination of basic goals and objectives of the organisation and the course or courses of action by analysing the strength and weaknesses of the firm and matching them with external opportunities and threats as illustrated in Fig. 2.1.

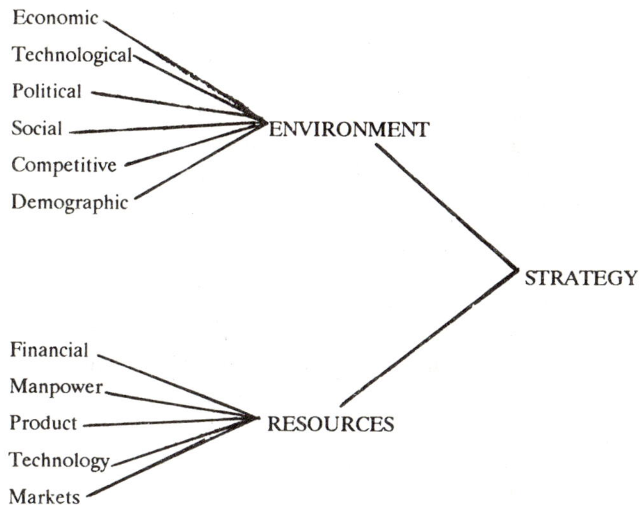

FIG. 2.1: Environmental and Firm's Resource Analysis

The strategy has been defined by D. Schendel and K.J. Hatten (1972) as "Strategy refers to the basic goals and objectives of the organisation, the major programmes of action chosen to reach these goals and objectives and major patterns of resource allocation used to relate the organisation to its environment".

Vencil (1966) has defined the concept of strategy as follows:

> The strategy of an organisation, or the sub-unit of a larger organisation, is a conceptualisation expressed or implied by the

organisation's leader, of: (i) the long-term objectives or purposes of the organisation, (2) the broad constraints and policies either self-imposed by the leader or accepted by him from his superiors, and (3) the current set of plans and near terms goals that have been adopted in the expectation of contributing to the achievement of the organisation's objectives.

Strategy formulation involves analysing environmental opportunities in the light of internal capabilities of the organisation, developing possible alternatives and evaluating them in terms of their respective contribution and finally selecting one or more alternatives for implementation. The decision framework of Simon (1960) is very helpful in understanding the process of strategy formulation. Simon has shown that the solution of any decision problem can be distinguished into three phases. First, intelligence activity phase which involves environmental analysis to identify problems to be solved in the light of opportunities available. Second, design activity phase which comprises formulation of alternative courses of action and evaluation of the alternatives for their respective contributions and finally, choice activity phase i.e. choice of one or more alternatives for implementation. Strategy formulation requires strategic decisions which are taken at the level of top management. The choice of appropriate strategy is necessary to have orderly and profitable growth of the organisation. Corporate strategy has mainly two aspects i.e. one formulation of strategy and second its implementation. Strategies should centre on pin-pointing the strong and weak aspects of the business and spelling out what actions are to be taken to eliminate weaknesses and to build on strengths.

Turnaround strategy is a carefully evaluated action plan which is aimed at stemming the declining trend in the operations of an enterprise through identification of causes resulting in performance decline and initiation of concrete steps for improved financial and productive results leading to normal growth of business. Turnaround strategy is aimed at what is to be done, who is to do it, how it is to be accomplished and when it is supposed to be completed. Turnaround strategy is required when there is a substantial and sustained declining trend in the performance of a unit normally measured in terms of profit. It may be caused by external factors and internal factors (discussed in Chapter 1). The turnaround strategy is aimed at reversing the trend of declining performance immediately and stabilising it leading to normal growth of the business in the long run. The thrust of turnaround strategy is either at increasing the operational efficiency or strategic decision or both.

The fundamentals of strategic planning are the same, however, turnaround strategies are shorter, more direct and subject to more frequent revisions. As the immediate objective before the turnaround leader is very simple: survive and return to positive cash flow. The choice of turnaround strategy would depend on various factors such as stages of sickness i.e. tending towards sickness, incipient sickness and the gravely sick, causes of sickness i.e. external or internal or both, operational performance gap, strategic gap etc. Sick units generally suffer performance gap. It may have operational performance gap or strategic performance gap or both. The operational performance gap is the difference between the actual and potential performance of the existing business. It has been found that most of the sick units suffer from the operational performance gap. The sick unit may suffer from the strategic gap also such as the problem of over-diversification, over-expansion and high leverage. The strategic gap is more critical factor in the choice of turnaround strategy. Hence, there is no single turnaround strategy that could be adopted for all sick units. Each case has to be studied and the various possible steps be assessed and tailored to suit the particular case.

The thrust of turnaround strategy would depend upon the magnitude of seriousness of the problem and various stages in a turnaround strategy. During the last stage of sickness i.e. gravely sick stage, our aim is to get the sick company to positive cash flow and ensure its survival. During this stage, drastic steps are required to be taken to keep the company 'survive'. Once the company is out of the red, the emphasis would be to stablise the positive cash flow and profit improvements and finally returning to normal growth stage. Therefore, turnaround would require less efforts and less resources, if it is detected and initiated at early stage of sickness.

The turnaround strategy should be appropriate in the light of limited resources available to a sick company. The turnaround strategy has two main aspects: (1) formulation of turnaround strategy, and (2) implementation of formulated strategy.

Once the management turnaround stage is complete, the viability analysis in terms of available resources — financial strength, market competitiveness and human resources — should be made. It would give the information about the stage of sickness. The sick company may fall in three general levels of sickness:

1. *Gravely sick stage*. In this case the very survival of a company is at stake.
2. *Incipient sickness*. This is stage in which the company is suffering from continuing losses and weak liquidity position yet that has not threatened the survival of the firm. But if the losses continue in future the threat to its existence is clearly visible.
3. *Tending towards sickness*. In this stage, the company is not sustaining its present business position in terms of market share, profit margins and hence profitability starts declining and return on investment is not satisfactory.

Apart from the above information, the viability study by the turnaround manager would provide information regarding the causes of declining performance of a troubled company, falling in any of the above stages. The analysis of level of seriousness of sickness and the evaluation of company's financial strength, market competitiveness, current strategic health and current operating health of the troubled company would help to formulate turnaround strategy.

Before formulating a turnaround strategy, the current health both strategic and operating of troubled company can be rated in a corporate health matrix as given below:

CORPORATE HEALTH MATRIX

Operational Health	*Strategic Health*		
	Good	Average	Poor
Good			
Average			
Poor			

The above analysis would indicate:

1. Whether turnaround strategy is required or not. For example, a company having both strong strategic position and operating position does not need a turnaround.
2. What type of turnaround strategy is required — strategic turnaround strategy or operational turnaround strategy or both. For instance, when there is a weak operating position and moderate or strong strategic position, operating turnaround strategies are usually needed.

The basic thrust of operating turnaround strategy is on increasing the operational efficiency of the firm. There may be three types of operating turnaround strategies:

1. Cost reduction strategies,
2. Revenue generating strategies,
3. Disposal of assets.

The choice as to which of the above strategy is to be adopted would depend on the stage of the operational seriousness of the company which can be judged from the rating of a company in a corporate health matrix. Cash flow projections and break-even point would also be useful in selecting the operating turnaround efforts required. For example, if the sales of the company are close to break-even point say 70 to 80 per cent, cost cutting strategies should be preferred. Because cost cutting strategies produce results more quickly compared to revenue generating strategies. If the sales of the firm are far below break-even point say 25 to 50 per cent, the revenue generating and asset reduction strategies are more appropriate. Because it is not easy to reach at BEP by reducing cost in this situation, so revenue generating efforts are required. If the company's financial position is critical, asset reduction strategy would be more appropriate.

Strategic turnarounds concentrate on divesting of that business which is not operationally viable and diverting the fund realised to finance the turnaround of viable unit. It is usually attempted by companies having strong operating position. Usually the combination of the above strategies have been found more effective particularly in case of gravely sick units. However, the results would be delivered only if they are successfully implemented.

STAGES AND STRATEGIES

A company goes through the various stages in pulling itself out of a crisis and finally restoring to healthy growth. The turnaround programme may commence at various stages of a company decline, it would vary depending upon the situation. If turnaround activity starts when the company has reached the stage of grave sickness, one is to go through all the stages of turnaround described below. If the symptoms of sickness have been detected in the early stages one may skip over some of the stages or at least move very rapidly through one stage to another. In many cases, very little time is to be spent in diagnosing the problems, and immediate action is important to keep the company survive. Therefore, the blending of activities and the overlapping of stages in a specific situation must be left to the judgement of the turnaround manager. Bibeault (1982) has described five stages of a turnaround:

1. The Management Change Stage.
2. The Evaluation Stage.
3. The Emergency Stage.
4. The Stabilisation Stage.
5. The Return to Normal Growth Stage.

It has been observed that most of the successful turnarounds in India as well as abroad (Khandwalla 1989, Bibeault 1982, Slatter 1984) went through the above stages of turnaround. However, the time span to overcome each stage varied dramatically. One of the best summaries of the turnaround stages was described by Robert Brown:

> "The first stage is to take the 'Big Bath'. The new manager comes in and takes everything that he can find — including the kitchen sink — and writes it off. He usually over-reserves so that he has some spread coming up on the outside. You're not thinking about anything but survival. He gets back tax money from Uncle Sam, as much as as he can. The 'Big Bad Bath' clears the way for the banks, the creditors, and the suppliers. You have laid yourself upon the table and told everybody how bad it is. From this point

on, it can only get better. And you have left yourself a cushion to make it better within the first year. The second cycle is the identification of the reallocation of resources. Generally, what you do is cut all the losers out and try to put all the emphasis on the winners. Capital expenditure-wise, management resource-wise, everything else goes to the winners. Get profitable, show profit, show progress. After you have done that and you have pretty much got out of trouble, you try to recapitalise. This is the third stage. And you do that along conservative lines — trying to get your short-term bank borrowings and all your money funded out in the long end of the market. Get it as long as you can so that you have got more 'breathability' in your balance sheet, so you have some money to work with and you have financial capacity to do something. Then it branches off into two areas, both of which are development-oriented. The last stage is either to go into the acquisition game or to innovate — make new products, design new things, enter new markets, and hopefully you are back on the growth curve" (Bibeault, p. 92).

The turnaround stages and strategies thereon which can be observed distinctly in most of the successful turnarounds are explained below:

Taking Charge

In 'taking charge' stage, attention is focused on understanding the problem and deciding to make fundamental changes to overcome them. At this stage the management realises that the company is in crisis and requires measures to stand it back on its feet. To come out of the trouble, management is replaced in most of the successful turnarounds since the majority of corporate decline has been attributed to poor management at the top. In one of the surveys, in more than seven out of ten cases, management has been replaced because they either could not cope with the problem or they themselves were the problems (Bibeault, 1982). In an another study of 42 successful turnarounds from round the world including 12 public enterprises and 30 private companies, out of 27 elements of turnaround, management changes at top level have been found in 93 per cent turnaround cases (Khandwalla, 1990, p. 21). It is found that the existing top management lacks credibility and hence cannot take drastic steps which are almost inevitable in a serious turnaround situation. Normally the turnaround manager is picked up from the outside since the outsider has the advantage of evaluating the situation more objectively and hence is in a much better position to take drastic measures. Management change can mean either replacing the existing top management or change in approach. Normally in most of the successful turnaround cases described in part II, the former has been adopted. Existing management of a sick unit is most unlikely to accomplish a successful turnaround for two reasons. First, they are the party to the present difficulties and second existing management is often emotionally involved with people and hence cannot take unpleasant and harsh decisions usually required in turnaround.

The viability analysis and preparation of action plan and its implementation is the key function of the new management team. The seriousness of the problem should be recognised before preparing the action plan. However, sometimes the stage of sickness is so acute that identification of problems and actions are performed simultaneously. Efforts should be made to identify the thrust areas requiring urgent attention to revive the unit. Once the critical areas for turnaround are identified and understood properly, a written action plan should be prepared and communicated upwards to the board for approval and downwards for implementation. It would enhance the credibility of the turnaround team and provide leverage to exercise effective control. Getting commitment from the parties concerned is the key for the successful implementation of turnaround action plan.

Survival

In this stage, necessary steps are taken to implement the action plan. Basic emphasis is laid on those activities which are necessary to ensure the survival of the company. The priority of activities to be implemented depends on the seriousness of the problem. In serious situations, top priority is given to stop the outflow of cash i.e. stop the bleeding. Cash management is considered the most important in this stage of turnaround. Necessary steps are taken to control cash flows i.e. to stop outflow of cash and to control the causes that result in negative cash flow. If the company is not facing alarming cash flow problems and faced with stabilising and improving profit performance, the areas where you can take action and achieve results fast are to be determined and put into action. These actions might be taken in the absence of a well-formulated strategy as the emphasis is to identify and divest those segments of business which are not contributing to cash flow. Restoring profitability and stabilising operations generally means shrinking back to those segments of business which can achieve good profits.

The focal point of turnaround strategy during this stage is to take all steps which are necessary to ensure its survival. It is just like an emergency medical surgery to the human body. Critical problems are identified and steps initiated to ensure survival and positive cash flow since it ensures the company's immediate survival and provides a foundation for profitable growth. Problems having turnaround leverage are given top priority. The technique of segmentation would be very useful and helpful in identifying the critical problems and to speeding up the formulation of turnaround plan. Segmentation means classifying the activities, expenditure, people, inventory etc. into A, B and C categories. Priority may be determined in terms of revenue, cost and problems, for instance, business activities can be classified into green i.e. viable, red i.e. non-viable and yellow i.e. border line cases. Expenditure can be categorised into absolutely needed for current, needed for day-to-day requirements and needed for future potential requirements. People can be classified into A, B and C categories representing people to be retained positively, better to retain meritwise and lastly to be retrenched. The segmentation of business activities, people, expenditure, inventory is to be made on the basis of information gathered by the turnaround manager.

The segmentation analysis would help to identify the critical problems where maximum efforts, time and resources are to be concentrated to ensure the survival of the unit and positive cash flow. The time to be devoted on the above analysis would depend upon the urgency of the situation and scale of business. Once the critical problems are identified and understood, turnaround action plan is to be prepared. It is found in various cases that action plans are cash flow plans. Top priority is given to stop the cash flow bleeding i.e. negative cash flows. In serious situations cash is the crucial factor during this stage in a turnaround plan as most of the sick units suffer from immediate cash problems. More emphasis is laid on operational turnaround plans compared to strategic turnaround plans as the latter require more time as well as resources to be initiated. Operational strategies can be initiated more quickly as they are related to internal actions. During this stage, planning and action can take place simultaneously. The possible turnaround strategies relating to finance, marketing, products and human resource, which may be initiated, are explained below:

(A) *Financial Restructuring*

Cash crunch is almost inescapable problem during this stage and hence it is requisite for the management to know the size and time of cash required. The preparation of cash flow projections would high-light how much cash and when it is required. Cash generating and conserving it, leading to positive cash flow, is the focal point during the survival stage. Top priority is given to stop the bleeding i.e. putting halt to the over flow of the cash since cash is crucial for the survival of the unit. More emphasis is to be laid to reduce the operational performance gaps. The following steps may be initiated to prepare financial action plan:

I. Take the control of the cash both inflow and outflow;
II. Analyse the cash flow problems; and
III. Finally, prepare financial action plan to solve the financial problems on permanent basis.

However, there is no single financial strategy that can be adopted for all turnaround cases. Each case has to be studied separately and the various possible steps should be assessed and tailored to suit the particular case.

Action plan should be based on cash flow projections. It should identify what is to be done, who is to do it, how it is to be accomplished and when it is supposed to be completed. Since cash is crucial for the survival of the unit, key problems that have maximum leverage on cash and hence on turnaround are to be identified and incorporated in a financial action plan during this stage. To generate cash as and when required as per projected cash flow statement, more emphasis should be laid on internal sources compared to the external as later require more time. However, operating cash flow is the best source of generating cash but not suitable during the survival stage as it also requires more time. Time is the crucial factor for the survival of the unit during this stage. Therefore, top priority is to be given to the balance sheet management. The possible financial strategies which may be adopted during this stage are as under:

1. *Rescheduling of Debts of Financial Institutions and Banks*
There are provisions of finance to be provided by the financial institutions to sick units for their revival provided they are found viable (Appendix). The financial institutions are IDBI, IFCI, ICICI and IRBI and state level financial corporations. These institutions also assist for rehabilitation in the cases of sick units and normally initiate viability studies if they have already given term loans earlier. The financial institutions and banks can be approached to grant reliefs as a package deal comprising:

(a) Rescheduling of old term loans;
(b) Funding of interest on old principal amount;
(c) Waiving of accumulated interest and penal interest on fresh term loans as applicable on soft loans.

2. *Settlement with Creditors*
Settlement with creditors, deposit holders and government bodies for payment of their dues is very important during this stage. There should be an understanding to prevent any legal proceedings against the sick unit for recovery of their dues in a phased manner. Negotiations should be made with the suppliers, vendors and employees for immediate relief in terms of cash by wiping out or getting some concessions in old debts and requesting more for on-going operations, asking for higher credit lines and strengthening the terms of repayment of debts. Kamani Tubes Ltd. is a case for illustration (discussed in detail in Chapter 8).

3. *Cost Reduction*
Special attention should be given to the cost reduction since they produce results more quickly than revenue generating strategies. The cost reduction programme can be carried out in all the departments by carefully scrutinising the working and the necessity of incurring or not incurring expenditures in these areas. During this stage emphasis should be on one time cost reduction programme. It has to be adopted after knowing where, when, and how much cost cutting is possible. Cash projections could be of assistance in analysing the above questions. Some of the important areas where cost cutting

actions may be initiated are listed below:

I. *Organisational Structure:*

(a) Reduction in management posts.
(b) Reduction in emoluments of posts.
(c) Tight approval procedures for recruitment.
(d) Elimination of some operating units and service departments.

II. *In Marketing Area:*

(a) Review of policy for travel and entertainment and reduction of expenditure.
(b) Freeze on advertisements.
(c) Modification of commission structure.
(d) Possibility of reduction in sales-promotion staff by appointment of agents/dealers etc.
(e) Reconsideration of sales discount or trade discount or cash discount.
(f) Distribution policy by owned transport instead of hired transport.
(g) Examining the location of godowns and warehouses.
(h) Examining the inventory holds in these godowns and reducing it where necessary.

III. *In Finance and Accounting Deptartment:*

(a) Elimination of unnecessary and voluminous reporting system.
(b) Centralisation of cash management for effective deployment of funds to needy departments.
(c) Tight control on more productive expenditure.

IV. *In Manufacturing Department:*

(a) By simplifying purchase procedures and reducing personnel employed therein.
(b) By providing production incentive schemes or rationalising them if already in existence.
(c) By exploring energy saving devices and reducing power consumption;

(d) By using better material, handling equipment and facilities.
(e) By carrying out work study and better job allocation to the people already employed and retrenching all those found surplus.

4. *Sale of Surplus Fixed Assets and Obsolete and Surplus Inventories*
The assets may be classified into assets to be retained, border line cases, assets to be sold, on the basis of their contribution to cash in short run. The decision for sale of fixed assets should be taken in the light of the true value of assets, the degree of the convertibility and the time spent for necessary conversion. It would help the management in knowing the immediate cash recovery from the sale of a particular asset.

5. *Effective Working Capital Management*
Emphasis should be laid on improving liquidity position through proper cash planning and control, management of receivables and payables and effective inventory management. Cash planning and control involves projecting cash in-flow and out-flow, managing cash in-flow and out-flow and arranging cash as and when it is required. In the area of receivables management, efforts should be made on turning receivables into cash. Causes of accumulated receivables are to be analaysed. These may be poor credit screening, product deficiencies, incorrect invoicing and ineffective collection procedures. Efforts should be made to collect the cash from debtors through negotiations and making payment of bills as and when they fall due. However, priority of creditors is to be decided keeping in view the size, age and other factors relating to credit outstanding. Inventory management is also to be given due weightage as it would help in reducing the inventory cost, generating cash and ensuring continuous and smooth flow of production. Inventory items may be classified into critical, not so critical and not critical for continuous and smooth production. Management must ensure that critical items are in the stock or in the pipeline. Emphasis should be laid on regular supply of such items on generous terms and not so much on prices. The not so critical items may be sold even at less margin but it would depend upon the size and time of the cash required.

The commercial banks may be requested to consider the following aspects:

I. To provide additional working capital facilities in the light of turnaround programme.
II. The shortfalls in the existing accounts may be transferred to working capital term loan account to be repayable on the basis of cash generation capacity of the unit.
III. Banks may be requested not to stipulate any margin or to fix up some normal margins on such advances until the unit turns the corner and starts cash generation.
IV. The old dues to the bank may be transferred to deferred term loan account to be repaid over a period of 5 or 6 years after moratorium of one or two years depending on the cash generation by the unit.
V. Negotiating for loan on a very low rate of interest.

The cash projections should be made on monthly basis. However, the daily cash projections are preferable and monthly cash projections are to be made an essential requirement. The object of daily and monthly cash projections is to have strong control over the cash i.e. cash inflow and outflow which is crucial factor during this stage.

(B) *Marketing and Product-mix Strategy*

Marketing strategies regarding pricing, product line and promotional efforts should concentrate on generating cash and reducing marketing cost. As the unit faces the problem of cash crunch during this stage, it should concentrate at strengthening the existing products in existing markets and distribution channels. Ineffective pricing policy as generally found in case of sick units may be on account of under-pricing strategy. The Neyveli Lignite Corporation (NLC) is a good case for illustration. Hence the problem of under-pricing is to be recognised and accordingly price strategy is to be formulated and implemented. Regarding product line, diversification beyond control may be one of the important factors of sickness, NELCO is an example in this regard. Hence dropping of products may be made on the basis of product contribution analysis. Each product is to be analysed in terms of its contribution separately. High margin products and low margin products are to be identified. The decision regarding dropping of poorly performing products should be made after proper analysis of the various aspects such as whether the sales volume of the product or product line is rising, stagnating or falling; whether the product is of high margin or low margin.

The above analysis would help to highlight the poorly performing product and would also help to generate cash by converting receivables into cash and saving on inventory, labour cost, overheads and disposing of machinery and the other surplus equipments used for the product or products being dropped.

Promotional cost should only be incurred on the products which generate cash immediately. The expenditure on building image, public relations and advertisements are virtually to be avoided during this stage. The amount saved may be used to promote sales in a number of other ways such as price reduction, increasing sales outlets, more margin to the wholesalers and retailers.

(C) *Human Resource*

Overstaffing has been found one of the major problems in the case of sick units. The management of surplus manpower and lay off of employees in divested activities are the basic concerns in this regard. The former may be managed by the manpower reduction strategy. It should be resorted to only when the survival of the unit is at stake on account of high amount of wages, since it is difficult politically and socially to retrench employees in most of the cases. An important aspect of this strategy is the retrenchment of surplus manpower and its management. It calls for evolving fair and acceptable separation, adequate compensation and effective communication both within and outside the unit.

Retrenchment orders are to be announced and executed at a time so that the uncertainty and anxiety among the remaining may be minimised. Appropriate notices should be given to all concerned. Retrenchment may take place at operational level, middle executives level and even at higher executives level. The method of categorising the employees into: (a) to be retained, (b) border line cases, and (c) to be retrenched, may be helpful in this regard. In several cases, the retrenchment strategy featured as one of the key actions initiated for turning around the unit, for instance ICIM, DVC etc. (fór details see cases discussed in Part II). Employees in divested operation is another problem. Efforts should be made to engage them in other activities or to get some suitable alternative employment. But it would depend on the number of employees of divested activities, their willingness to be transferred and opportunities available. NELCO is a good illustration where 300 people idle on the radio division were trained and fully employed elsewhere successfully.

Profit Stability

This is a settling down stage. The company starts taking those actions which ensure an acceptable rate of return on the funds invested. The emphasis shifts from liquidity management ensuring survival to concentrating on improvement in profitability by running the existing operations more effectively, efficiently and repositioning the company for medium term growth. Cost reduction, divestment and retrenchment measures can solve only short-term cash problems. Cash required for medium- and long-term growth can be ensured only through sustained profitability. Hence during this stage, the emphasis is laid on profit improvement with stability by making investments in profitable activities and running its current operations more effectively. It involves a planned withdrawal from unprofitable products, services, market segments and developing profitable alternatives from both profitability and future growth point of view. Information system is also introduced to monitor the performance since the absence of such system has been found one of the major causes of sickness. It would help the management to detect the problem in time and respond quickly. It would enable the management to be sensitive and responsive to things that are going on either direction — good or bad.

The emphasis shifts from ensuring cost reduction for survival to profit improvement with stability having a reasonable rate of return on assets employed. The management starts looking beyond the day-to-day problems of cash requirement. The activities of the company from cash to cost accounting, purchasing to production, designing of products to distribution are to be thoroughly analysed with a view to have significant improvement in efficiency and effectiveness resulting in higher profits. Opinions of customers and employees about the company should be considered. Strategies are to be formulated and implemented emphasising the following aspects:

(a) Profitability coupled with positive cash flow, since only sustained profitability can make available the long-term cash required for growth of the unit. One time cost reduction and disposal of fixed assets can solve only short term cash flow problems.

(b) Profit margin improvement along with sales volume growth.

(c) Increasing of efficiency through effective systems of control both in financial and non-financial areas. Management information system can be helpful in this direction.

(d) looking for the business areas which are more attractive from the future profitability and growth point of view.

The various possible strategies relating to finance, marketing product mix and human resource which may be adopted during the profit improvement stage in turnaround are discussed as under:

(A) *Financial Strategies*

Financial strategies should concentrate on profitability improvement by increasing profit margin, financial restructuring, cost control, introducing effective control system on cash, inventory and debtors. The following financial strategies may be useful during this stage:

(i) The emphasis in managing working capital should be on improving profitability by effective cash flow planning and control i.e. prudent financial management policies. Steps are to be initiated to reduce the amount involved in bills receivables and inventories. This should be done after taking calculated risk associated with the various components of working capital.

(ii) Management should develop financial control systems namely cash control, cost control, budgetary control. Profit improvement is to be achieved by systematic programmes rather than one time cost reduction. Inventory management is to be intensified, and overhead cost is to be reduced on the basis of cost analysis. Effective control over purchases, inventory, debtors, and cash should be exercised. Effective accounting information system should be developed relating to cost control, budgetary control, product profitability analysis, responsibility accounting. Steps are to be initiated to achieve efficiency in manufacturing, such as increasing labour productivity, proper maintenance of plant and machinery, transportation facility etc.

(iii) Financial restructuring followed during survival stage should be pursued vigorously during this stage also. Unit should start relying on its own financial resources rather than external ones. Negotiations with financial institutions and banks for financial assistance on continuous basis is an essential requirement.

(B) *Marketing and Product-mix*

On the front of marketing and product-mix, various actions concentrating on profit improvement resulting in reasonable return on investment may be adopted. These are as under:

1. Concentrating on developing the strong products and eliminating the weak ones.
2. Searching high return and high growth markets for existing products; minimising administrative expenses on marketing.
3. Stabilising marketing expenses;
4. Introducing higher profit margin products but it should be made only when marketing opportunities are available.
5. Rationalising pricing policies while determining the prices of the products, pricing practices of industry should not be ignored.
6. Efforts should be made to bring the marginal category products in profit earning category.

Product Mix: The emphasis of product strategy should shift from pruning the unprofitable products to scrutinising the existing products on the basis of cost and profit margin of each product. It should concentrate on dropping marginal products, pushing existing products, identifying more profitable products and introducing low risk products. The new products should be introduced only after analysing and exploiting the potentiality of the existing products. In this regard, the life of the existing product is given due weightage. If the new product is to be marketed to the same markets, similar group of customers through same channel of distribution and similar kind of selling efforts, it may be profitable but the company should move slowly and carefully during this stage.

(C) *Human Resource*

Human resource strategies should concentrate on disciplining, motivational and welfare measures. Management should identify willing and able employees who will rise to the challenge and retrench those who will not support your turnaround efforts. But this action should be taken keeping in view the raising of performance of the organisation. The performance can be raised by improving the people mix. The case of NELCO is an example where the above strategy was adopted during turning around of the unit.

Efforts should be made to resolve the issues relating to centralisation, decentralisation and organisational conflicts. Profit centres may be introduced with decision-making power within the overall objectives laid down by the turnaround managers. The magnitude and direction of organisational conflicts have to be recognised and dealt with. The turnaround managers must manage these conflicts in a decisive manner. Two way communication and participative approach in goal setting would help in creating the feeling of profit consciousness among employees. This would result in a feeling of belongingness and encourage every individual to put in his or her best efforts for the organisation.

Growth

Once the trauma of survival and profit stability is over, the turnaround manager is faced with a new challenge of maintaining consistent growth in profitability. It requires concentration on long-term planning leading to sustained growth in the long run. The emphasis of growth strategies should be on revenue growth coupled with profit margin in the long run. Planning for growth should be balanced with resources available and other constraints of the company. The management should concentrate on broadening the base of existing business, identifying new markets and products resulting in fast growth in sales with high profit margins, sound capital structure and transforming the enterprise culture to build a momentum for future growth. The strategies to be followed at this stage are dealt upon below:

(A) *Capital Restructuring and Financial Management*

The objective of financial strategies should be to make funds available for long-term requirements with a view to maximise owners wealth. They are to be based on risk-return analysis.

The various financial actions which may be initiated are as under:

(1) Designing of capital structure ensuring profitability, solvency, liquidity, flexibility and controlability.
(2) Faster growth and higher return investment opportunities are to be identified. Environmental scanning and capital budgeting techniques may be helpful in this direction.
(3) Prudent working capital management ensuring liquidity and profitability. It requires estimate of working capital requirements and effective and efficient use of estimated funds. Investment in working capital should be adjusted in accordance with change in sales.
(4) Financial information and control systems should be introduced to monitor the performance of the unit periodically.

The various financial management techniques such as fund flow and cash flow analysis, financial ratios, standard costing, marginal costing, differential costing, budgetary control, inventory models, responsibility accounting, daily sales outstanding, ageing schedules, conversion matrix etc. may be used to monitor the performance of the enterprise.

(B) *Marketing and Product-mix*

Marketing and product strategies should concentrate on increasing sales of existing products, proper product mix, introducing new products and seeking opportunities in new markets. The emphasis should be to increase the market share of existing products and new products by identification of new markets and initiating additional promotional activities. But the pace of growth in new markets should be kept within manageable limit of the enterprise. The products which require huge capital to operate in profitable zone, and large amount of risk capital which is beyond the capacity should be avoided. The enterprise needs to be more responsive to market requirements and competitive during this stage. It should pursue a strategy of developing technological competence by seeking modern and relevant technology. This has to be deliberately pursued if the enterprise is to be responsive to customers and competitive in the market which is an essential requirement for sustainable growth in the long-run.

(C) *Managing Human Resources*

The management of human resources becomes more significant during growth stage in turnaround of a unit. Special attention is needed to manage people by following positive and responsive personnel policies, investing in development of workforce and motivating them to contribute their best. It requires more efforts to motivate and have a proper development of human resources. The level of motivation and productivity of employees and the behaviour of employees and trade unions are affected by the policies and practices of human resource management of the unit. Hence, the management should follow such positive personnel policies and practices that inculcate positive attitude resulting in better performance. The compensation and welfare programmes are to be modified in the light of long-term planning for growth. They should be inter-related and consistent with long-term business objectives i.e. revenue growth coupled with profit margins. Examples where such policies have shown positive results are DVC, NELCO, NLC.

Apart from various motivational measures, the management should concentrate on developing the workforce through proper training at all ranks and identification of committed individuals who will be required for the enterprise to grow in the long run. NELCO is an example where committed employees were identified and proved very successful in turning around of the unit. Training and development of employees needs special attention since it has been found one of the critical aspects of human resource strategies of successful units. Opportunities for training, self-development, education and career development programmes are some of the important components of human resource development. Promoting corporate culture should be the part of human resource management as it is the crucial factor for successful growth of the enterprise in the long run. The various aspects of promoting corporate culture are: transmitting the organisation mission to all employees; merging of the employees with the organisation, greater participation in decision-making, effective communication and a climate of openness. AFT has corporate uniforms that are worn by every employee including the executive head, thus inculcating the team spirit. Positive corporate culture inculcates the feeling of belongingness and encourages every individual to give his best performance. It gives a senses of purpose and direction to the individual. Finally, the pressure of working hours condition, inadequate staffing in relation to work should be identified and action be initiated. It requires long-range manpower planning and constant review of policies.

3

TURNAROUND REQUIREMENTS

Multiplicity of factors are involved in the turnaround of sick units. A long list of such factors can be prepared from the extensive experiences available on the turnaround of the sick units in India and abroad. A few observations regarding the key requirements for successful turnaround are presented below:

Bob Brown has aptly summarised the key turnaround factors as under:

> "You have to have four key elements to make the turnaround work. You have got to have the willingness. This means that the new man who is brought in to do the turnaround has to have absolute control. He has to report directly to the board, but he has to have the maximum flexibility that is given to any management. You cannot manage a turnaround by committees. It is strictly a star business, and you have to have a board that is willing to go along with that. The second thing is that he has to have something to work with. There has to be an economic reason for the business to be there. In other words, if you are making buggy whips, you can be the most efficient buggy-whip maker in the world; but if there is no demand for buggies, you should recognise that, get out of the business, and get into something else. The third key element is the money and resources to turnaround, to become a competitive entity. And the final ingredient is the motivation of people. You have to be able to attract and motivate top people in the key areas in which you are making the turnaround" (Bibeault, 1982, p. 111).

Ratan Tata, Chairman, National Radio and Electronics Company Ltd. has described the factors behind NELCO's turnaround as under:

> "I do not think there is any one area which can be defined (pin-

pointed). Certainly, as in all such turnarounds, effort of top management has played a major role. The second aspect is management focus in the sense of control over cash, setting of targets. Never before has there been this focus. If you look at NELCO's bad years, it is because some management factor went out of control. Where we have failed in the past is in managing our day-to-day business. Third, management of cash has always been an important factor in our business. We have always been short of cash. This is not a capital intensive, but a working capital intensive sort of activity. You do not revolve your money fast, you do not use it fast and you are in trouble. Financial restructuring played a very important role in the turnaround, because cash was a major problem. Without it we could not support the growth we have. Lastly, there has been a tremendous marketing thrust" (*Business World*, April 11-24, 1988, p.62).

M.M. Sinha, Chairman, Kumardhubi Metal Casting and Engineering Ltd. (KMCEL) points out:

"The revival of KMCEL has been possible because of a dedicated team of management deputed at Kumardhubi and vast resources of Tata Steel which were made available for this stupendous task when needed" (Sinha, 1985).

Richard Madden, Chairman, Potatch Corporation, USA says:

"There are three factors which affect all business, but which are more noticeable in a turnaround. There are people aspects; there are the business aspects of total competitiveness; and there are financial resources. When you start to look at these three factors, you can tell a lot about decline, turnaround and sustained growth (Bibeault, 1982, p.111).

In an American study about key factors in a successful turnaround, improved management processes and motivation aspects received 71 per cent of the first mentions as the key factor; competitive resource aspects (a viable business) received 17 per cent and financial resources aspects received 12 per cent (Bibeault, 1982, p.112).

Lee Iacocca who saved Chrysler Corporation of USA from

bankruptcy summarises the key factors in a successful turnaround as under:

> "In the end, all business operations can be reduced to three words: People, Product and Profits. People come first, unless you have got a good team, you cannot do much with the other two" (Iacocca, 1984, p. 176).

Mr. S.K. Mukherjee, the President and the Chief Executive, NELCO says:

> "NELCO turnaround strategy was three pronged: first, tie up the capital requirement; second change the organisational structure, and third, induce a sense of motivation and a corporate purpose" (*Business World*, April 11-24, 1988).

Goodman Stanley J. (1982) has described six key factors of successful turnarounds:

(a) Getting ready (The will),
(b) Building the team (The vehicle),
(c) The power of bifocal planning (The road map),
(d) Turnaround strategies (The motor),
(e) Motivating the team (The fuel),
(f) Monitoring performance (The pilot).

The analysis of these few observations stated above and the various studies conducted abroad and India indicates that a large number of factors are involved in successful turnarounds. However, there are certain factors which have been observed frequently in most of the successful turnarounds. The commonality of certain factors exists irrespective of the nature of the business and the environment or culture in which it operates in most of the successful turnarounds. These are:

1. Potential Viability of the Unit.
2. Motivated Top Management.
3. Timely Availability of Adequate Finance.
4. Effective Management Information System (MIS) (*discussed in detail in Chapter 4*).

The most important is the need to develop a culture of business turnarounds by recognising that downwards are part of the business operations.

POTENTIAL VIABILITY OF THE UNIT

Potential viability of the unit is a basic requirement in determining whether a sick unit could be turned around or not. It is important to assess whether a sick unit can attain viability in a reasonable time with reference to the profitable use of the company assets for existing and new activities. Viability on commercial basis should be the main criterion for undertaking turnaround of a sick unit. Only potentially viable units should be undertaken for turnaround as it is very difficult, if not impossible, to turnaround the non-viable units. A viability study, therefore, has to be conducted to determine whether a unit is potentially viable or not.

The general principles involved in viability studies are indicated by the factors affecting viability in a sick unit. These normally vary among companies, industrial groups and institutions. However, the approach to viability study has to be based on the analysis of post-operations of the unit with a view to determine its strength and weaknesses with regard to the various functional areas i.e. marketing, production, personnel and finance. The viability study should be carried out under three major heads: (a) Market Analysis, (b) Technical Analysis, and (c) Financial Analysis.

Market Analysis

A market analysis should contain a brief description of the market, methods of transportation, existing rates of transportation, channels of distribution and general trade practices. The analysis should include past and present demands including determination of quantity and value of consumption as well as the category of products being manufactured by the unit which are likely to be needed by the consumers. The competitive position of the products such as selling price, quality and market practices of competitors should be indicated. An estimate of future demand of product or products and product share of the market considering the demand, supply, competitive position etc. should be projected.

Technical Analysis

The technical analysis has to throw light on the technical feasibility regarding the manufacturing of the product or products in the light of the future demand. It should estimate the cost and funds needed to support it. The technical analysis should contain a review of techniques of processes to applied and other infrastructure support needed in the rehabilitation programme. The technical study in effect should be able to project the production costs in the light of the future demand and market situation.

The performance of the machinery and equipment and the capacity utilisation should be reviewed in the light of the future demand and if there are any modifications/extensions of the plant needed should be brought out. The technical analysis should also consider the availability of raw materials in the light of the future demand and the location of sources of supply, terms of payment and continuity of supply. The study should also estimate labour requirements and the break-down of direct and indirect labour and supervision costs required for the manufacture of the products. If there are any waste products and other ecological factors, and methods of disposal of waste should be brought out.

Financial Analysis

Market analysis makes possible to estimate the gross income at selling price. From technical analysis, the manufacturing cost is computed. To this, the cost of selling, administrative expenses, depreciation, interest on short-term and long-term borrowings and other recurring expenses are added. It should be possible then to estimate the net operating profit and the net return after the deduction of taxes.

An estimate of long-term funds requirement and the working capital required to finance current assets, and inventory must be brought out. The inventory comprises raw materials, spares and stores, semi-finished and finished products. It is to be noted that larger production and sales may result in increased accounts receivable due to credit being given to customers (say 60 to 90 days) and this in turn leads to liquidity problem or lack of adequate cash. It would, therefore, be necessary to prepare a cash flow analysis to project balance sheet, profit and loss accounts for a few years. Mode of repayment of loan with interest can then be planned and indicated as part of the viability study.

There are five key requirements (Bibeault, 1985, p.117) for a business to be worth turning around where the basic viability of the sick unit is in doubt. These are: (1) Positive Cash Flow, (2) Sales Volume Umbrella, (3) Competitive Equipment, (4) Competitive Location, and (5) Awareness of Changes in the recent past and near future.

Reserve Bank of India in its revised guidelines for reliefs and concessions to sick units by banks and other agencies (See Appendix) laid down that viability on a commercial basis should be the main criterion for undertaking the rehabilitation of a such unit. It should be adopted for identifying units to be put on a rehabilitation package. For this purpose potential viability of a sick unit is defined as under:

> "A unit may be regarded as viable if it would be in a position, after implementing a relief package spread over a period not exceeding seven years from the commencement of the package from the banks, financial institutions, Government (Central/State), Government agencies, shareholders, labour, suppliers of goods and services and other creditors, as may be necessary, to continue to service its repayment obligations as agreed upon including those forming part of the package, without the help of concessions after the aforesaid period. The repayment period for restructured debts should not exceed ten years from the date of implementation of the package".

The above definition brings out two points clearly regarding the viability of a sick unit. First, the unit should not need any reliefs and concessions after 7 years and should be able to service its repayment obligation without the concessions after the aforesaid period and secondly, repayment period for all restructured debts should not exceed 10 years.

Certain broad parameters have also been evolved for the grant of reliefs and concessions by banks and other agencies as part of the packages for the rehabilitation of potentially viable sick industrial units. These parameters should be kept in view while drawing up programmes of rehabilitation. The basic purpose of these parameters is to have some uniformity in the matter of reliefs and concessions to be extended for rehabilitation of sick units. Concessions and reliefs within the framework of these parameters would not require to be referred to the Reserve Bank of India for prior approval. Even the prior approval by the RBI for extending reliefs and concessions by commercial banks beyond the parameters fixed by it as part of the packages for rehabilitation of sick units has been withdrawn (*Economic Survey, 1990-91*, p.53). Details of RBI's revised guidelines for reliefs and concessions to potentially viable sick units are given in Appendix.

The viability status of 2,42,584 identified sick units as on December 31, 1988 is given in Table 3.1. The analysis of table indicates that 93.2 per cent of the sick SSI units and 44.2 per cent of non-SSI sick and weak units were not viable for revival. Bank credit blocked in non-viable sick units was as high as 72.5 per cent (Rs. 1550.81 crores) in the SSI sector and 33.6 per cent (Rs. 1867.03 crores) in the non-SSI sector. About 60 per cent of the total viable sick units were already brought under nursing programme till the end of December, 1988.

TABLE 3.1: Viability Position of Sick/Weak Units – End December, 1988

(*Rs. Crores*)

Category	Sick SSI Units		Non-SSI Sick & weak units		Total	
	No.	Outstanding Bank Credit	No.	Outstanding Bank Credit	No.	Outstanding Bank Credit
1	2	3	4	5	6	7
1. Viable units	13033 (5.4)	471.92 (22.0)	679 (33.8)	2419.83 (43.5)	13712 (5.7)	2891.75 (37.5)
2. Non-viable units	224080 (93.2)	1550.81 (72.5)	889 (44.2)	1867.07 (33.6)	224969 (92.7)	3417.88 (44.4)
3. Viability not decided	3460 (1.4)	118.27 (5.5)	443 (22.0)	1277.40 (22.9)	3903 (1.6)	1395.67 (18.1)
Total	240573 (100.0)	2141.00 (100.0)	2011 (100.0)	5564.30 (100.0)	242584 (100.0)	7705.30 (100.0)
(a) Units under nursing programme	7788	361.17	418	1603.40	8206	1964.57
(b) As percentage of viable units	(59.8)	(76.5)	(61.6)	(66.3)	(59.8)	(67.9)

Note: Figures in brackets show percentage to total.
Source: *Economic Survey, 1990-91*, p.52.

MOTIVATED TOP MANAGEMENT

As discussed in Chapter 1, there is fairly wide consensus that poor management is the prime cause of sickness in industry. If poor management is the key cause of decline, then dedicated competent top management may go a long way towards turning around the troubled units. Studies in India as well as abroad suggest that effective management is the key to the successful turnaround of sick units. In an American study by Bibeault (1982) about the key factors in turnaround success, the dedicated management and motivation aspects received 71 per cent of the first mentions as the key factor. Khandwalla (1989) based on case studies of five public sector units and four private sector units, identified the committed and credible top management and its style as one of crucial factors in turning around a sick units.

There are several examples in India where top managers and significant change in their management styles succeeded in turning around the sick units. For example, Sylvania and Laxman, a severely sick company in 1977, was turned around by Mr. Ragu Raj who was appointed as new Chairman of the company in 1978. Enfield India Limited which lost over 25 per cent on sales in 1976-77, was turned-around by Mr. Sankran. The important aspect in both cases is that Sylvania and Laxman and Enfield India operated in fairly competitive industries during their periods of turnaround. It is also observed in both cases that there was a significant change in the style of top management during the period of turnaround.

The National Radio and Electronics Company Limited (NELCO), which was considered a dead duck, was turned around by Mr. S.K. Mukherjee, who took over the reins of the company in April 1986 as its President and Chief Executive. The Rs. 69.66 crore turnover in 1987 recorded a 34 per cent growth in sales, the accumulated losses were wiped out and there was still a modicum of profits to transfer. It was the result of a happy combination of vision and mission of top management. The vision of company's Chairman Ratan Tata and the missionary zeal with which his Chief Executive, Mr. Mukherjee translated it into reality. Ratan Tata mentioned "I believe that the losses we suffered in the eighties were purely a function of the then management changing the complexion of NELCO. We were trying to do too many things. We launched too many products on flaky assumptions. We made too many commitments. Basically we got a case of indigestion. Everything was looked at short term. In a way, a lot of the kind of fabric, we had tried to build in the company — putting in a base of technology and creating capability was destroyed. And this is what Bobby (S.K. Mukherjee) has been trying to rebuild. It is his job to effect the turnaround, I am there in a supportive role", (*Business World*, April 11-24, 1988, p.60).

S.K. Mukherjee, NELCO President and Chief Executive explains his own role differently. "It is Ratan Tata who has been its principal architect. We are a set of charged-up people out here. My boys are working their guts out and they are having fun while doing so. We just took this bunch of people who had stayed on during the troubled times, people who believed in the company asked them for the impossible. And Lo and behold they delivered. That's the NELCO story, that's the turnaround" (*Business World*, April 11-24, 1988, p.61).

Kumardhubi Engineering Works (KEW), which collapsed totally in September 1979 and remained closed for 5 years, was taken over by TISCO Management in August 1984 and was successfully revived under the leadership of Mr. M.M. Sinha, Chairman, Kumardhubi Metal Casting and Engineering Works (KMCEL). Similarly, Metal Box (Nigeria) was successfully turned around by Kuldip Puri, who took over the reins of Metal Box (India) in 1985 resulting in posing a very pertinent question: "Can Kuldip Puri turn Metal Box around" (*Business World*, August 1985, p.44). Metal Box once counted as a Blue Chip Company with a Rs. 135 crores turnover and employees strength of 7000, was eventually on the brink of bankruptcy. Kuldip Puri took the revival of this company as a challenge. The leadership quality and credentials of Kuldip Puri contributed not only to halt the slide down in earnings, but reverse it. The last two quarters in 1985 saw upward trend in earnings and the company earned a net profit of Rs. 10 millions in the year ending March 1986 compared to the losses of Rs. 100 millions and Rs. 60 millions over the last two years. This was a tremendous turnaround, of course not yet complete. It was just a starting.

The turnaround of Bihar Alloys Steel Limited (BASL) is another example of how a perennially sick company was turned around within a short time by taking appropriate measures in a systematic way under the leadership of Basant Kumar, the head of the Jhawars group. When the Jhawars took over BASL in January 1987, a mini steel unit manufacturing alloy steel it was in the deep red. Within one year, both production and turnover were gone up by 50 per cent (57299 tonnes) and Rs. 63.28 crores in 1987 and the company made a small net profit of Rs. 1.19 crores after many years. An optimistic Basant Kumar said: "We set the ball rolling and are working hard to maintain the tempo. The goal is to reach one lakh tonnes of steel in three years from now" (*Business India*, March 1988, p.65).

Tithwal Mills was running in losses between 1957 and 1968 but started making profit in 1969 under the leadership of a young executive who joined the company as a P.A. to Sethji and later became its Chief Executive. The Fertilisers and Chemicals Travancore Ltd. was chronically in the red until 1981-82. It had accumulated losses of Rs. 66.86 crores with a share capital of Rs. 125.46 crores in 1981-82. Capacity utilisation remained continuously low (below 50 per cent). N.B. Chandran, who took over as Chairman and Managing Director in April 1983, succeeded in turning around FACT. The first sign of a major turnaround came in 1983-84, when the company made a profit of Rs. 10.54 lakhs. It continued to earn profit in subsequent years and won the National Productivity Award 1985-86 for its performance in capacity utilisation and Europe Award 1988. There is a consensus that Chandran played a significant role and was key figure in turning around FACT.

Even in the public sector, there are numerous examples where top management led to the successful turnaround of sick units. For example, the revival of Damodar Valley Corporation (DVC) under the leadership of P.C. Luthar. The revival of DVC was crucial to the entire belt in the eastern region, four integrated steel plants and the economy in general. P.C. Luthar, who was appointed as Chairman of DVC on 4th August, 1980, achieved turnaround within two years. The Corporation registered a dramatic upsurge in the performance under his determined efforts and style of management relating to discipline, accountability and dynamic welfare. He firmly believed that discipline and accountability flow like water from the top to the bottom. If these principles are not seen at the very top then they would never be seen at the bottom. His concept of dynamic welfare enabled him to secure the support and commitment of majority of employees. He spent three quarters of his time in the field talking to the workers and even their families to know the problems faced by them. With Luthar's dedicated efforts and style of management, power generation went up by over 60 per cent within one year. The

performance award. The plant was expanded and modernised resulting in improved quality of its product.

Mr. M.K. Raju who took over as part-time Chairman in July, 1972, was instrumental in turning around Hindustan Photo Films Ltd., a leading loser public sector unit in 1972. the HPF had accumulated losses of Rs. 22 millions even before it started production and had a cash loss of Rs. 26 millions on sales of Rs. 44 millions in 1971-72. By 1976, there was a remarkable improvement in sales turnover rising from Rs. 4.4 crores in 1972 to Rs. 20 crores in 1976 and capacity utilisation from 53 per cent to 110 per cent over the same period and reached at break even. The products of HPF began to enjoy a high degree of acceptance within the country and started exporting X-ray films to East Germany.

In the case of Hindustan Copper, Bharat Aluminium Corporation (BALCO) and Burn Standard, the determined management succeeded in drastically reducing the extent of sickness. Hindustan Electrical Engineering Company Ltd. (HEECOL) had seen rising sales until 1974 but a decline set in thereafter. Mr. Gupta took over as Chief Executive in 1973 and by mid-1975, the company started earning profit and was poised for a major expansion (Chakraborty and Sen, 1980). L. Vasudev, Chairman and Managing Director of Madras Fertilisers Limited who assumed office in February 1987, succeeded in turning around the Madras based public sector unit. From a net loss of Rs. 26.05 crores in 1987-88, the company earned a pre-tax profit of Rs. 11.1 crores during 1988-89 and sales turnover increased from Rs. 160 crores to Rs. 270 crores during 1987-88 to 1988-89. It had been possible because of dedicated efforts and professional approach of top management towards tackling of the problems which pushed the company in red. It is confirmed by the statement of L. Vasudev 'MFL tightened its belt and adopted a professional attitude towards problem solving' (*Business India*, November 1989). Travancore Cochin Chemicals (TCC), Kerala State Undertaking, was turned around in 1980-81 by Mr. T.N. Menon, who took over the management as Chairman and Managing Director in mid-1978. In 1977-78, the company's net operating to sales percentage was 17 per cent, versus the private sector industry average of 15 per cent. The company broke even in 1979-80. In 1980-81, it made a profit of 10 per cent on sales and in 1981-82 it earned 17 per cent on sales. In 1981-82 the company's net operating profit to sales percentage was 24 per cent for the company and 12 per cent for the industry (Khandwalla, 1990).

From the examples cited above and case studies discussed in Part II, it can be seen that determined and motivated managers with a sense of mission has been instrumental in reviving most of the sick units both in public sector as well as private sector. Sense of mission starting from top played a major role in the dramatic turnaround in performance achieved by the companies cited above. Leadership qualities and styles constitute the most important part of successful turnaround manager. The personality traits and commitment to the enterprise are of crucial significance in turning around of sick units. The vision, dedication and integrity of managers determine whether there is proper management or mismanagement. Turnaround manager is an architect as well as an implementer of turnaround strategy. Hence, he should be tough-minded and have the qualities of self-confidence, decisiveness, objective orientation and an impatience to get something done. He should have certain skills such as an entrepreneurial instinct coupled with professional management skills, a broad business experience not necessarily in the same line and good negotiating skills to negotiate with the parties concerned such as creditors, bankers, labour unions etc. The turnaround leader's personal style is more important during the period of turnaround than at any other time in corporate life. Personal traits inspire confidence in the ultimate survival of the sick unit. Bibeault (1982) in a survey of eighty one turnaround chief executives has ranked the personal characteristics of turnaround leaders as under:

1. Objective-oriented,
2. Self-confident,
3. Maintains positive outlook,
4. Inspired confidence in others,
5. Innovative and creative,
6. Highly visible and active.

Iacocca (1984) has pointed the following factors which constitute effective management:

1. The quarterly review system. It works for several reasons. First, it allows a man to be his own boss and to set his own goals. Second, it makes him motivated on his own. Third, it helps new ideas to the top. Fourth, it keeps people from

getting burried and finally it forces a interaction between a manager and his boss and helps to control the business by making the turnaround manager aware of the situation.

2. Decisiveness
3. Building the team and ability to motivate.

The new management is likely to be perceived with indifference by many insiders if he is an insider and with suspicion if he is an outsider. Therefore, it is very crucial for the new management to establish its credibility as quickly as possible to win the confidence and motivate the workforce. The ability to know how to delegate and motivate, how to look for pressure points and how to set priorities makes the turnaround leader strong. People can be motivated through effective communication. In a corporate life, they are to be encouraged to make contribution to the common cause and to come up with better ways of doing things. The managers should listen the workers if he is to motivate the people who work for him.

Schendel, Patton and Riggs in their study Corporate Turnaround Strategies (1976) observed that "Management actions appear to dominate the upturn phase. Turnarounds appear due much more to management actions than to favourable environmental events and the key to upturn is explicit action by management".

Sound management and effective leadership had been at the root of most of the successful cases of turnaround. The finding of a suitable manager is perhaps the most difficult task of sick units, particularly where it is found that sickness has been attributed to bad management or the management's integrity and honesty has been doubtful. In India, there appears to be shortage of top level management personnel. The sick unit which requires better management becomes a victim of this acute shortage. Managers of proven ability are usually absorbed by the healthy units. The sick units usually get a superannuated person with practically no stake for his career. It is hard to find good manager and very difficult to be loaned or deputed from a working industrial unit. The government and the financial institutions have now realised and agreed that a pool of experience turnaround managers should be constituted, but it is as yet not in existence. Needless to say that the greatest need of a sick unit is an effective top manager who can put the unit back on rails again.

TIMELY FINANCING

Timely availability of adequate cash is the third key requirement of successful turnaround of sick units since they invariably face cash crisis. Sick units may not have cash even to meet their normal operating expenses. How much cash and when it is required would depend upon the stage of sickness i.e. tending towards sickness, incipient sickness and gravely sick. If the unit is in the gravely sick stage, cash is required for immediate relief ensuring its survival and stabilising operations restoring health. It is just like a patient who is in need of blood transfusion.

The estimate of size and timing of finance required should be made on the basis of cash flow projections over a period of time. Financial action plan should be prepared. Funds may be arranged both from the external and internal sources. Raising of funds from the external sources would depend upon the potential viability of the sick unit and the credibility of its management. Various financial strategies such as rescheduling of debts, settlement with creditors, sale of surplus fixed assets, cost reduction, effective control over working capital etc. (discussed in Chapter 2) may be adopted to make the required funds available in time either from external or internal sources or both. Financial institutions, banks and creditors can play a significant role in providing funds to the viable sick units. Various provisions have been made regarding reliefs and concessions to sick units by financial institutions, banks and other agencies while evolving rehabilitation package (for details see Appendix). Management may negotiate with the bankers, financial institutions and creditors to get adequate funds on timely basis. Efforts should be made to get assurance not only for immediate cash required but also for longer term financial requirements. Getting assurance from the funding agencies would depend upon the feasibility of turnaround action plan. Timely disbursement of agreed funds by the financial institutions and banks is of great help in reviving a sick unit.

4

MONITORING PERFORMANCE

Effective management information system is a pre-requisite for monitoring the health of industrial units. It becomes all the more essential in a turnaround situation, since the turnaround manager needs information fast about the company's cash flow position and its prospects, operating cost, customers, competitors, employees and its control systems in order to take decisions that give the company a fighting chance for its survival. Therefore, the information and reporting system has to be designed to meet the requirements of industries during implementation phase for new units which are being set up and for production phase when they are in operation. An information system is simply an organised method by which decision-makers in an organisation are presented with needed information in the appropriate format at the appropriate time in order to improve the quality of their decisions. The nature of the information, format in which it is presented and timing varies not only among organisations but also from one decision-maker to another.

THE PROBLEM

Substantial empirical work, has been carried out on the causes of growing phenomenon of industrial sickness, and diverse views have been expressed (Argenti, 1976; Ross and Kami, 1973; Kharbanda and Stallworthy, 1986; Altman, 1983; Allsop, 1977). One of the basic causes of the growing sickness in industry on which there is a fairly wide consensus is the poor management, coupled with inadequate information and reporting system, resulting in poor monitoring, both during the implementation and operational phases of projects. In an analysis of 223 sick industrial projects, poor management has been identified as the most significant factor which contributes over 43 per cent to the sickness in industry (Srivastava and Yadav, 1986). On further analysis, it is observed that lack of proper information and reporting system, especially accounting information, is the significant factor associated with poor management that contribute to sickness. The several deficiencies noticed concerning the information and reporting system are: (a) no or poor cash flow planning; (b) no or poor costing system; (c) no or poor budgetary system; and (d) the poor reporting of faults, break-downs and sales. The lack of adequate information and reporting system decreases the ability of the management seeing the approaching disaster, with the result corrective measures are not taken in time. It results in management's inability to respond to changes which then becomes a major cause of sickness, and keeps on increasing from incipient stage to grave situation (see Fig. 1.2 in Chapter 1).

While examining a large number of sick units, it has been observed that information and reporting system in the organisation is usually poor. There is considerable variation even when there is some form of reporting between the companies in the same industrial group and between industrial groups also. The reports are not submitted to the management in time and are seldom carefully scanned for variance analysis.

The importance of detection of sickness at the incipient stage as also the need for proper co-ordination between commercial banks and term lending institutions in formulation and implementation of rehabilitation packages has been emphasised from time to time. The government, the reserve bank of India, commercial banks, and financial institutions have been striving hard and spending a sizable amount of resources for preventing the spread of industrial sickness and for revival of sick units. The setting up of Board for Industrial and Financial Reconstruction (BIFR) is a major step enabling intervention at an early stage, and taking remedial measures. However, the results have not been satisfactory as the number of sick units, both large and small, is increasing at an alarming rate. Therefore, there is a need to evolve a more effective monitoring system so that sickness can be stemmed earlier, and units are made productive.

INFORMATION AND REPORTING SYSTEM

Keeping the above in view an attempt has been made in this chapter to design a Management Information System (MIS) to help monitoring the health of industrial units, both during implementation, and operational phases. It has been designed to achieve the following objectives:

(a) Detecting early warning signals and symptoms of sickness, both during implementation and operational phases, so that preventive action can be taken in time.
(b) Keeping a watch on the extent and rate of deterioration while remedial measures are being evolved and implemented.
(c) Once the unit has been turned-around successfully, the monitoring system should ensure that the unit gains strength and does not slip back to the stage of sickness.

The methodology for designing MIS is divided into four stages: (i) Designing of format of reports; (ii) Filling up of reports; (iii) Analysis of data; and (iv) Making decision, followed by actions.

Information System for Implementation Stage

Poor implementation usually results in cost and time overruns in projects and causes sickness (Korgaonkar, 1988). Cost overruns have become a common phenomenon, particularly in the case of the public sector projects. Delays in 58 major projects cost the national exchequer Rs. 15,897.90 crores as on 1 January, 1987 (*Hindustan Times*, 1988). This comes in the way of executing projects, which become uneconomic and non-viable, particularly when the magnitude of cost overrun is higher. Cost overruns lead to budgetary deficits, upset the effective economic planning, and tell on the economic development at the macro level.

Very often no effort is made in developing a regular monitoring system of implementation, and the extent of slippages in different activities are not brought to the notice of the management resulting in poor response and corrective measures. Poor implementation results because of : (a) inadequate planning of various phases of project implementation; (b) poor anticipation of bottle-necks; and (c) lack of contingency planning to overcome bottlenecks.

Therefore, the emphasis has to be on the following information during the stage of implementation: (i) The schedule of implementation; (ii) Expenditure incurred with break-up under various heads; and (iii) The progress made towards raising of resources. It would help keep a watch on various phases of project implementation and to anticipate bottlenecks and plan for alternative actions in time avoiding delay in completion of projects.

Planning for Project Phases

A project plan can be presented through a network of activities or through a bar chart. The bar chart method is simple and convenient. An example for the planning of manufacture of brakes by the bar chart method is given in Fig. 4.1. It is important to keep watch on various phases in the implementation and to anticipate bottlenecks and plan for alternative actions well in time, so that completion of project is not delayed. A network of activities on a project is, however, a better approach for planning. It considerably helps in arresting the time and cost overruns as illustrated in Fig. 4.2 where the activities and project milestones have been related with financial expenditure on project. Such plans and periodic review are very useful in the follow-up of implementation phase.

Contingency Planning

It aims at providing alternative approach when an activity or a group of activities in a project gets delayed. For instance, if one of the venders defaults in providing components or the contractor fails in construction, alternative solutions are to be anticipated. Splitting orders or parallel activity planning are well-known steps to be attempted. To anticipate bottlenecks and plan for alternative actions is the task of the management. It has been noticed that projects, which have been successfully implemented made good use of contingency planning.

A good reporting system and periodic reviews during implementation phase is very useful in preventing time and cost overshoots. Network planning or bar chart approach has proved very useful in estimating delays leading to timely corrective measures.

Information System for Operational Stage

Information system during operational stage has to be such as to provide a quick check on the health of a unit in the periodic review. It should make use of key variables of information, such as capacity

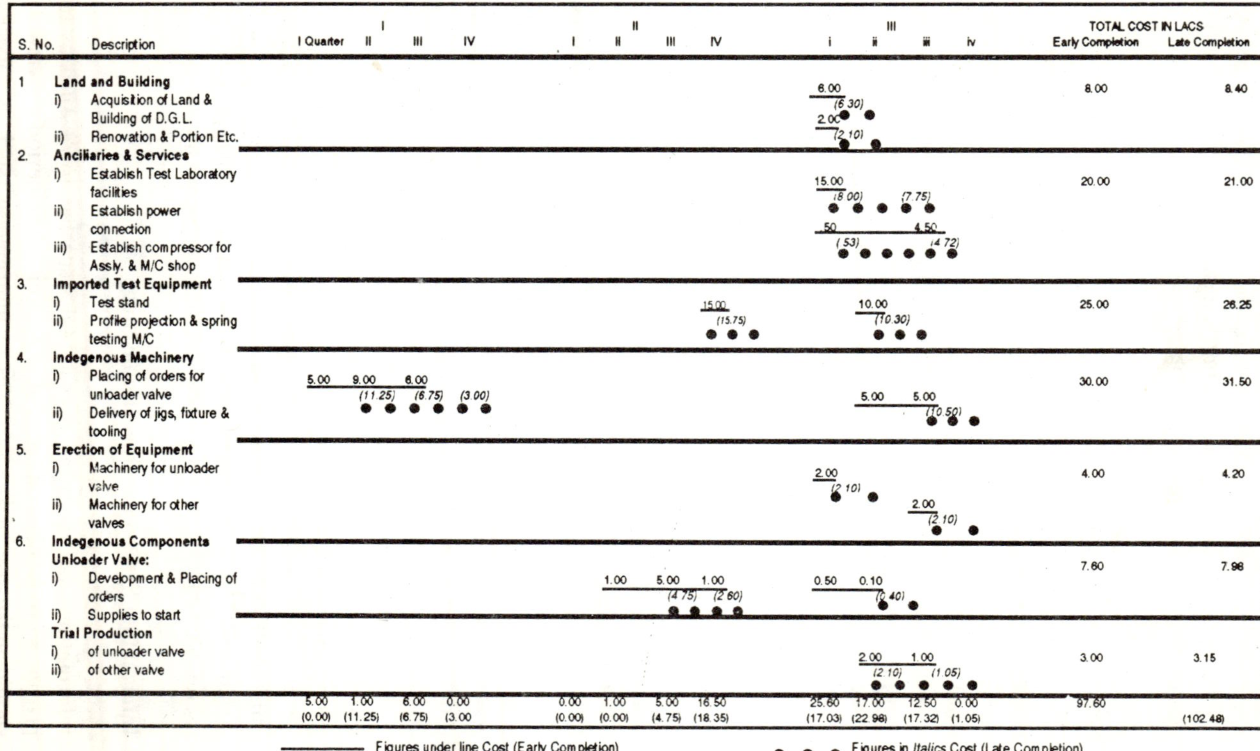

FIG. 4.1: Bar Chart for Grau Brakes

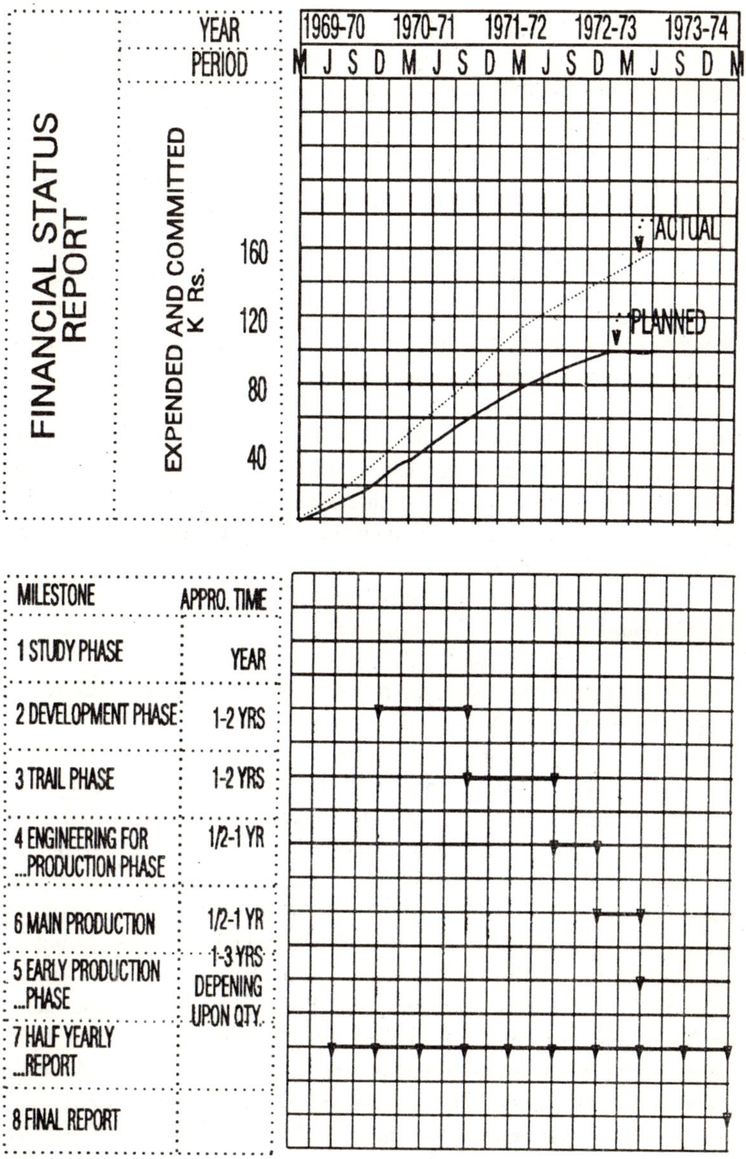

FIG. 4.2: Project Milestones and Financial Expenditures

utilisation, factors of production, cost of production, sales, cost of sales, administrative and other expenditures, and, finally, parameters relating to liquidity, solvency, and profitability of a unit. These variables can broadly be grouped into: (i) basic data; and (ii) operational data.

Basic Data

This is about the project, its promotors, management, capital structure, etc. The basic data about an industry can be organised in several groups. A computer file for each group can be created when computerisation of MIS is undertaken. Even in manual maintenance, it would be convenient to make changes when required in a group. The basic data can be maintained in the following groups: (a) Project location and promotors' details; (b) Particulars of project, collaborators' and their details; (c) Cost of project; (d) Capital structure; (e) Details of share-holders and equity base; (f) Financial assistance obtained from financial institutions and banks; and (g) Schedule of repayment to lenders.

Operational Data

The operational data should be reported preferably every quarter or may even be half yearly depending upon the nature of activity and the requirement of the monitoring system. This should consist of details relating to the activity concerned with the items and quantities produced during the quarter, the details of profit, and cash management during the same period. It is possible to lay out an information format to report in these three aspects of the operational data; however, the contents will have to be listed depending upon the nature of the operations in a unit. The operational data should be meaningful to enable critical appraisal and assessment. It should have the key elements of information. Eventually, a data-base has to be built and a computerised filed created for each one of these elements of information and kept updated. This should be done for each industrial group. The operational data have to be adequate to meet the requirements of appraisal in respect of financial, operational, and technical working of the industrial unit. The information should be adequate to plot graphically the trends of growth in respectively areas over several quarters.

KEY INDICATORS OF HEALTH

The information system should be used to appraise the health of a unit. The following key indicators based on the use of operational data are identified and used to assess the health of an industrial unit.

(a) Physical indictors as reflected by the key elements of information, signals, and symptoms in the company's performance in the quarterly reports;
(b) Graphical indicators plotted taking the total production, profitability, capacity utilisation, etc., and their trends during several quarters;
(c) Data from commercial banks on transactions in the quarter, and
(d) Use of Multiple Discriminant Analysis (MDA) score as indicator of health.

Physical Indicators

The physical indicators include selected data on the plant performance, capacity utilisation, important financial ratios and their changes, if any. In the early stages of sickness, the physical indicators appear in the form of signals. An example of this is given in Fig. 1.1 in Chapter 1. The decline in market value of shares, inefficient management practices in the areas of finance, production, marketing, and labour relations do provide indications of growing mis-management. However, occasional plant break-downs are not of much consequence, but when they start recurring, the malfunctioning has to be recognised. The plant and equipment starts getting aged and needs replacement. Because of the break-downs, plant utilisation starts decreasing and the hours lost become very significant physical indicators of health and consequently capacity utilisation decreases. Plant break-downs are quite normal in old textile, jute, and engineering industries, where technology is becoming obsolete and operational cost is constantly increasing. Replacement programmes of old equipment is not worked out systematically in spite of the fact that depreciation is worked out each year by the companies. Replacement of obsolete technology is also necessary as the break-even point constantly changes while capacity utilisation shows a downward trend. In fact, updating of technology is a basic requirement of industry and has to be planned very systematically.

Important financial ratios and their changes, if any, can also be good physical indicators. The values of selected key ratios can be worked out and guidelines can be laid down as a measure of performance. A combination of financial variables can be a good guide towards estimating the proneness to sickness. An example of this in respect of profitability and liquidity is shown in Table 4.1. A combination of technical factors like plant and equipment utilisation and operational factors like availability of critical raw materials and skills is shown in Table 4.2.

TABLE 4.1: Guide for Estimating Proneness to Sickness

Profitability	Liquidity		
	High	Medium	Low/Lack
High	Poised for Growth		Expanding (Need Watch)
Medium	Healthy Idle Cash (Need Watch)	Healthy Usable Operations	Over Trading (Need Watch)
Low/Loss	Liquidation (Need Watch)	Contracting Business (Need Watch)	Sick

TABLE 4.2: Availability of Critical Raw Materials and Skills

Technical factors (plant and equipment utilisation)	Operational factors (raw materials availability)		
	Excellent	Medium	Poor
Excellent	Healthy	Needs watch	Sick
Medium	Healthy	Sick	Very Sick
Poor	Needs watch	Sick	Very Sick

Graphical Indicators

The graphical indicators are really the trends which can be plotted over a period of time, extending from one to two years where data are noted in every quarter and put on a graph. The trends in financial, operational, and technical parameters during two or three quarters preceding the quarter for appraisal can give sensitive indication regarding the health of the unit. The parameters can be selected in the field of capacity utilisation, liquidity, solvency, profitability, production, and sales. An example of trend analysis in respect of key financial parameters (Yadav, 1986) is given in Fig. 4.3.

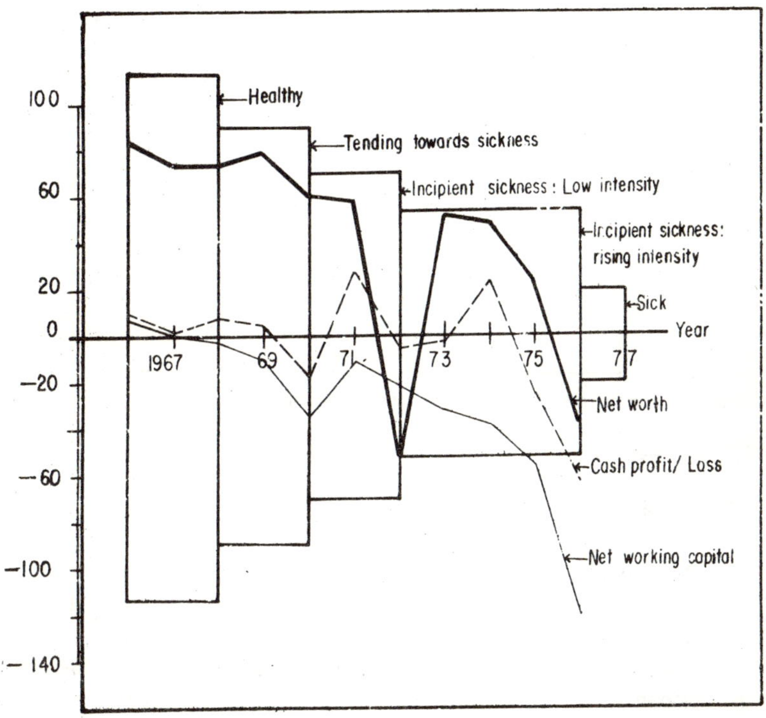

FIG. 4.3: A Sick Unit from Textile Industry

Commercial Bank Data

The variation in working capital and imbalances in bank borrowings are also very useful indicators of health of a unit. The uncontrolled swings can provide first vital information to the banker and also to the management if they monitor it and are keen to find reasons for it. However, such data can be obtained only from commercial banks of the units concerned or by other lending agencies. The data should be obtained on a periodic basis from banks and variations noted. A format is illustrated in Fig. 4.4.

Name of the bank	Nature of facility	Description and value of security	Margin %	Drawing power	Amount outstanding	No. of overtradings
1	2	3	4	5	6	7

Remarks: Indicate irregular accounts, if, and reasons thereof.

FIG. 4.4: Monthly Data from Commercial Banks on Borrowings

MDA Score

The Multiple Discriminant Analysis (MDA) model (Y = 19.8927 EBIT/TTA + .0047CA/CL + .7141 NS/TTA + .4860DA/TOE) (Yadav, 1986), and the extended MDA model (Srivastava and Yadav, 1986) where '*Z*' score has been calculated for different industrial groups can be a very sensitive indicator of the incipient sickness in an industrial unit. The MDA score can be used to review the past state of the health of a unit up to six years from the date it is declared sick. If the data in respect of variables used in MDA model are available for any new unit, the function can be used in assessing and monitoring the health of that industrial unit.

The predictive power of the model has been examined over a period of six years prior to the data of sickness for the initial sample and summarised in Table 1.10 in Chapter 1.

Table 1.10 clearly indicates that the model is accurate in predicting industrial sickness though with decreasing probability. The fall in the predictive accuracy of the model is logically understandable taking into account the long period that elapses, because the indications of the ratios become less and less clear as the lead time from the date of sickness increases.

The model is applied to a series of additional samples of sick and non-sick industrial units taken both from homogeneous and non-homogeneous groups of industries to judge its validity and effectiveness. These samples are taken at random irrespective of size, fiscal year, and age of units. The importance of test samples cannot be overemphasised since the real efficiency of the model lies in predicting the sickness of a unit which is not used to develop the parameters of the model. The model has been successfully used in predicting sickness in the nine industrial groups comprising over 20 units in each. The nine industrial units studied are: textile, jute, paper, chemical and pharmaceutical, iron and steel, electrical, engineering, sugar and rubber. The predictive accuracy of the model is summarised in Table 1.11 in Chapter 1.

Empirical results indicate that the predictive accuracy of the model is very high in homogeneous and non-homogeneous groups of industrial units, though the overall performance of the model in the case of homogeneous group is better, compared to that of non-homogeneous group. It may be due to the homogeneity of the industry group to which the model is applied.

MONITORING HEALTH

The early stages of sickness can be detected if the signals which originate in the areas of financial, technical, and operational of an industrial unit are carefully noted and catalogued. It can be attempted through a process of monitoring the financial status of the firm in respect of working capital, cash losses, and erosion of net worth. The financial data of 11 sick industrial units randomly selected have been analysed and presented in Table 1.7 in Chapter 1 where the time gap between the first appearance of sickness and 100 per cent erosion of net worth is shown. The first appearance of sickness is measured in terms of negative working capital and cash losses though there are other financial and non-financial parameters also to measure it. The analysis of the data in Table 1.7 shows that the working capital becomes negative to start with, followed by cash losses. The 50 per cent erosion of net worth takes seven to eight years. This period is quite critical. At this stage, the unit enters into a stage of grave sickness because the landslide from 50 per cent erosion to 100 per cent erosion in net worth follows in less than two years. From the above, it comes out that a unit at 50 per cent erosion of net worth is in a grave state of sickness. This also reveals that sickness in the early stages can be identified through a monitoring process of the working capital, cash losses, and erosion of net worth up to 15 per cent as this state of affairs generally lasts for two to three years.

There are ample signals and symptoms, both financial and non-financial (as shown in Fig. 1.1 in Chapter 1) available in this period of sickness which should be adequate for the management to take necessary action. The information and reporting system has to be organised to take note of these events. Figure 4.5 illustrates the stages where signals and symptoms of sickness should be noticed and health of the unit put under observation. It is in these early stages of incipient sickness that remedial measures can quickly restore the normal working of the unit and prevent further deterioration. Inspection procedures need to be tightened and periodic reviews enforced to improve performance. Experience has shown that rehabilitation of a sick unit is time-consuming and results in loss of production and finance. In fact, the dictum *prevention is better than the cure* can be applied effectively if information system based on key indicators is organised. The monitoring can be done effectively if there is a data bank in the industrial unit. It is necessary to build a data bank for different industrial groups in financial institutions, State level finance corporations, and other financing and non-financing bodies. Such a data bank would greatly help in the process of project appraisals and monitoring of implementation and operational phases of projects. The data bank must also have data on the cost of plant and equipment, supplies and types of technology available in the appropriate areas.

Management Information and Decision Analysis System

Monitoring of project progress during operational phase can be made continuous. It is then possible to detect signs of sickness if and when they appear. A database in respect of selected ratios from financial, technical, and operational areas will be needed for each industrial group. The MDA model can be used in determining the

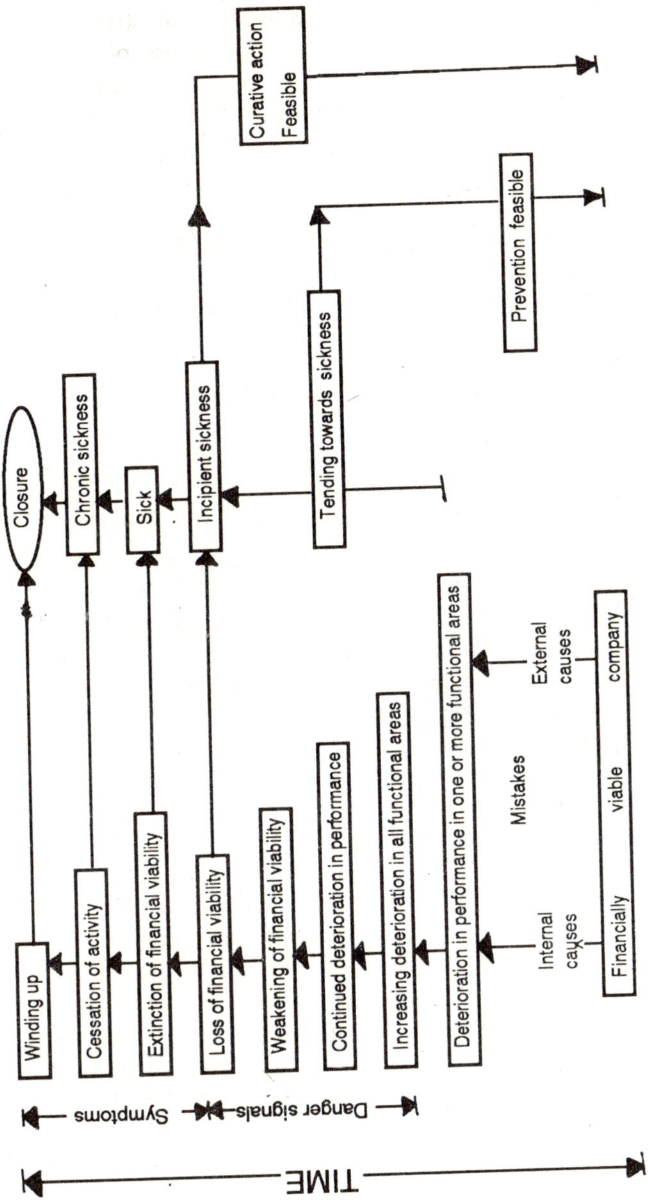

FIG. 4.5: Stages of Sickness

health score, and to examine the state of health of an industrial unit to be investigated. Using trend analysis and making use of other indicators, it would be possible to continuously monitors the health of industrial units with a high degree of reliability. A flow chart for this decision analysis system is given in Fig. 4.6. The appraisal reports can be brought out periodically from this computerised management information and decision analysis system (MIDAS). In each industrial group, it is possible to evolve quantitative norms in respect of chosen ratios for acceptable performance. A comparison of healthy and not so healthy units can also be made, and a reporting system designed for various levels of decision-making. The reporting system so organised for different industrial sectors can also be useful as a pre-budget industry report to the government from financial institutions, State level corporations, and industrial research organisations in guiding the basic taxation and subsidy policies of the government for good industrial growth in the country.

A layout of the reporting organisation at institutional level for various levels of decision-making is shown in Fig. 4.7. Such a feedback is likely to prevent chaotic changes in government taxation and subsidy policies. Once the information system is organised, it is possible to provide reviews for important operational functions of the industrial unit like production, marketing research, development and planning, etc., and link them up with resource requirements for the purpose of strategic and tactical planning. It can prove very useful in monitoring the performance of industrial units and in helping the corporate institutions in keeping a watch on the industrial growth in various sectors of the economy.

A careful analysis of MIDAS would enable the firms to have an idea of the stage of sickness/otherwise that deserves attention based both on financial and non-financial parameters and other criteria made use of in the analytical framework. In fact, the meetings/seminars would serve as the place wherein exchange of thought would take place between the representatives of firms, financial institutions, and government agencies who are looking at broader aspects of growth at different levels, to outline, discuss, and thrash out various aspects pertaining to industrial, financial, fiscal, and monetary policies that are necessary for the growth of firms that constitute the backbone of the economy. As suggested in the

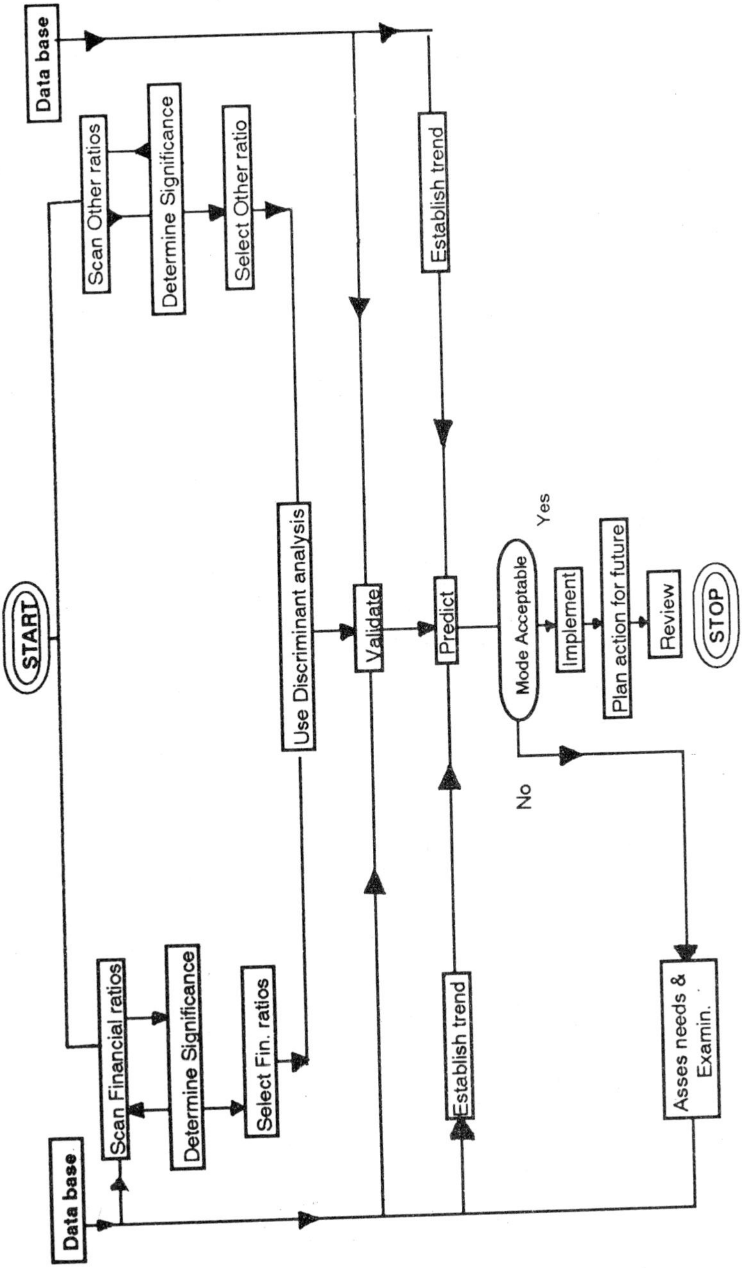

FIG. 4.6: Decision Analysis System

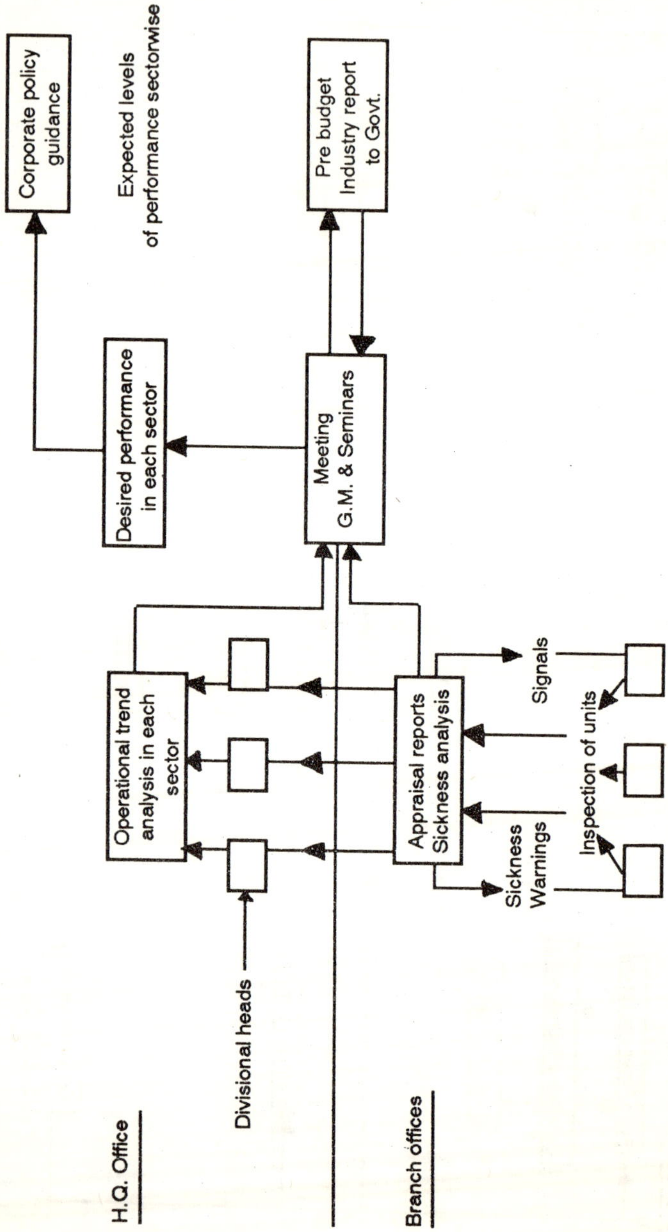

FIG. 4.7: Management Information & Decision Analysis System (MIDAS)

on-going analysis, the provision of a data bank is going to be of great use in focusing attention on various points that are discussed in different meetings/seminars for the purpose of improving the health of such units. The nation is at double loss when the firm becomes sick, one, the capital at its command remains unutilised, and, the build up of a fresh unit requires further investments which are to be provided from the scarce resource. In order to bring forth the optimal use of the available resources, MIDAS is going to prove effective in more than one way by utilising the opportunity of inter-exchange of views in the best interests of the units, financial institutions, the government, and the economy as a whole.

MIS in Management Process

Once the information system is organised, it is possible to provide reviews for important operational functions of the industrial unit like production, marketing, research, development and planning etc. and link them up with resource requirement for the purpose of long-term or strategic planning or short-term like tactical planning. A block representation of MIS in management process is shown in Fig. 4.8. Such computer outputs periodically are needed for the purposes of improving the productivity of the organisation and to consider malfunctioning if any because of organisational overlook in different areas.

It has been said, "*If You Want to Manage Business Well, Manage its Future, and to Manage Future, You Have to Manage Information*". There is an explosion of knowledge. New materials are being developed and better technology is becoming available as science progresses. It is possible to examine various alternatives from cost-effectiveness point of view if new technology or materials/ machines become available and compare the strategic and tactical plans in the light of the objectives of the organisation. A computerised output can help this process as shown in Fig. 4.9 and enable the management to plan better future and thus ensure *Growth*. Computerised MIS in large organisations can thus help and improve the decision-making in strategic, tactical and operational planning in industries.

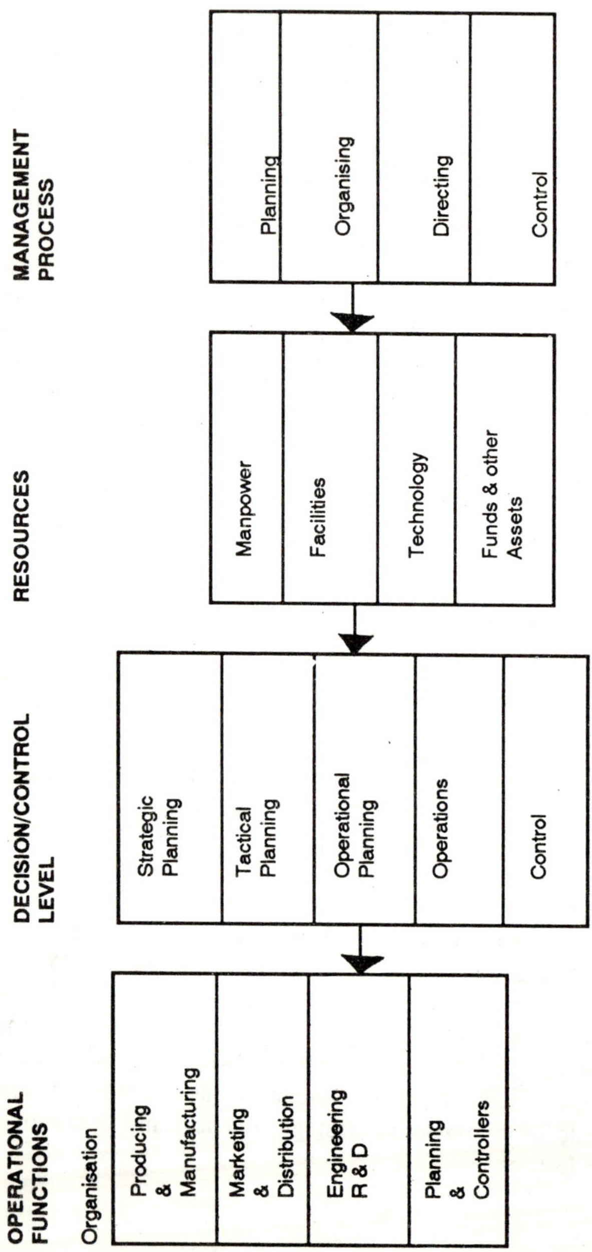

FIG. 4.8: MIS in Management Process

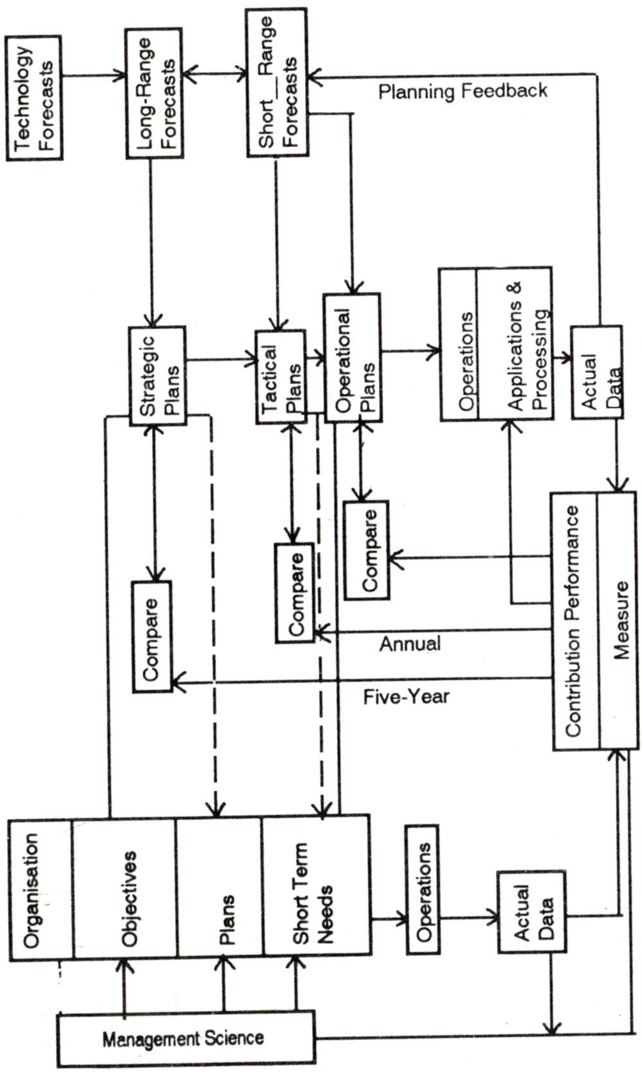

FIG. 4.9: Overview of MIS

PART II

CASE STUDIES

5

THE NATIONAL RADIO AND ELECTRONICS COMPANY LIMITED (NELCO)

The National Radio and Electronics Company Ltd. reported a turnover of Rs. 67.82 crores and a net profit of Rs. 73.61 lakhs in 1987 wiping out its entire amount of accumulated losses and transferring a small quantity of profit (Rs. 6.23 lakhs) to general reserve in the balance sheet. In spite of continued growth in sales, the performance of the company in terms of profitability has not been satisfactory till 1986. Since 1976-77, the company always had the accumulated losses except for a period 1982 to 1984 and of course in 1987 and 1988 respectively. The company suffered a loss of Rs. 1.25 crores and Rs. 26.91 lakhs in 1985 and 1986 respectively in spite of increasing trend of sales. it declared dividend only in 1984 in nearly last two decades. However, the company, which was known for its unsatisfactory performance and strained industrial relations in Tata Empire has effected turnaround in 1987 clearing all accumulated losses in one stroke in 1987 and achieved improved performance — 43 per cent growth in sales and 35 per cent rise in operating profits during 1988. The financial profile of the company over a period of ten years is given in Table 5.1. How was this miracle accomplished?

Background of the Company

NELCO was established as a private company on 31st August, 1940 at Bombay with technical collaboration of E.K. Ltd., England for a period of twenty years to manufacture a wide range of electronic goods—Radio, Radiogram, and Radio components, and other electronic products. It was converted into a Public Limited Company on 28th May, 1949. Initially, it was known as the National Ekco Radio and Engineering Company Ltd. It was started with a paid-up equity capital of Rs. 3 lakhs in 1940 which has increased to Rs. 6,97,94,000 in March 1990 (See Table 5.1). The management of the company consists of a Board of Directors headed by a Non-Executive Chairman and a Managing Director. Prior to April 1986, the Company had a functional based organisational structure. Since 1971, Ratan Tata has been associated with the Company as Non-Executive Chairman.

The Company is producing a wide range of products starting from radio to computer. Automated Drive Control System and Electronic Exchange (EPABXS) System based on C-Dot technology. The products are classified under three categories — consumer products, industrial systems and office automation. These products have been launched by the company over a period especially in the seventies and early eighties. In 1977-78, the company received an industrial licence for the manufacture of Data Acquisition and Control Systems and started its production in 1979. In 1980-81, the company obtained a licence to manufacture mini-computer/micro processor based systems which became fully operational from August 1981. During 1984-85, the company embarked on a programme of manufacturing and marketing a range of office automation products such as plain copiers, word processors, personal computers. It received an industrial licence for the manufacture of 2000 sq. m. of Printed Circuit Boards (PCBs) and double-sided plated-through hole PCBS were manufactured. In October 1986, the company introduced its first colour TV set under the brand name "Blue Diamond". It got the licence for the manufacture of Electronic Exchange Systems in December 1987 and started its production using indigenous technology developed by C-Dot. Presently, the products are sold under the trade-mark 'NELCO'.

In 1975-76 the company collaborated with Schlumberger Ltd., a French company which acquired 36 per cent of NELCO's equity shares. The collaboration was in the areas of Test Instrumentation and Data Acquisition Systems. However, it could not go well as the Schlumberger was interested only in the upper ends of both markets which did not have any demand in India. Though the company still has a 27 per cent equity stake, but is in the process of diluting it.

TABLE 5.1: Financial Profile of the National Radio & Electronics Company Ltd. (NELCO)

(Rs. in lakhs)

	Ending March 1980	(15 months) June 81	June 82	June 83	June 84	(18 months) Dec. 85	Dec. 86	Dec. 87	Dec. 88	(15 months) March 90
Net sales	1081	1187	1901	2309	3113	6201	5359	6781	9821	14598
Operating expenses	1055	1199	1736	2133	2907	6078	5018	6347	9171	13319
Depreciation	7	14	17	18	23	52	67	79	82	112
Operating Profit	19	(−26)	148	158	183	71	274	355	587	1167
Non-operating income/loss	51	31	56	40	104	243	64	184	195	(−10)
Earning before interest and taxes	70	5	204	198	287	314	337	539	781	1157
Interest	50	69	75	121	173	439	364	463	648	1055
Net Profit/Loss	20	(−64)	129	73	90	(−125)	(−27)	74	113	45
Profit Retained	20	(−64)	129	73	71	(−125)	(−27)	74	113	45
Equity Capital	174	174	174	174	218	218	318	444	565	695
Net Worth	74	10	139	212	326	464	529	720	946	1114
Long term Debt	92	9	150	106	261	592	953	1420	1534	1010
Current Liabilities	729	739	925	1358	1855	2892	2894	3880	5163	7765
Total Tangible Assets	894	837	1215	1674	2441	3899	4312	5962	7590	9854
Current Assets	769	732	1062	1453	2086	3050	3323	4831	6399	8558
Defensive Assets	418	362	608	926	1380	1681	1995	3007	4035	4958
Net Working Capital	67	(−7)	137	95	231	158	429	952	1286	793
Inventories	378	370	454	527	706	1369	1328	1824	2364	3600
Debtors	367	278	528	826	1327	1360	1821	2674	3655	4242
Cash & Bank Balances	42	52	64	78	26	264	119	258	275	264
Market value per Equity Share of Rs. 100 — High Rs.	41	101	195	410	370	430	320	131	175	700
Low Rs.	41	40	82	160	210	300	100	115	97	600

Source: The Stock Exchange Official Directory, Bombay.

The Decline

The company had a chequered history in terms of profitability till 1986 (Table 5.1). It was only constant infusion of funds by Tata which could keep NELCO alive. The company always had accumulated losses since 1976-77 to 1986 except for the brief period — 1982-84 because of variety of reasons. These were poor management, lack of vision, topless for nearly 15 months, introducing a wide range of products without adequate funds and marketing base, poor products with 80 per cent rejects, lack of product focus, centralised marketing system for all the products i.e. the same marketing team was selling products ranging from a small set of Rs. 100 radio to a Rs. 100 lakhs industrial electronic system, no R & D department, trading company approach, paucity of working capital, proliferation of new ventures at the expense of primary business, strained industrial relations. Ratan Tata termed the Nelco a case of a indigestion. He says "I believe that the losses we suffered in the eighties were purely a function of the then management changing the complexion of Nelco. We were trying to do many things. We launched too many products on flaky. assumptions. We made too many commitments. Basically we got a case of indigestion. Everything was looked at short-term. In a way, a lot of the kind of fabric we had tried to build in the company — putting in a base of technology and creating a capability — was destroyed" (*Business World*, April 11-24, 1988). The above statement clearly spells out the causes of declining profitability of the company, in spite of its continued growth in sales.

Turnaround Strategies

The company had turned the corner and cleared its all accumulated losses in one stroke in 1987. It had been possible on account of induction of Mr. S.K. Mukherjee as the Chief Executive of the company in April 1986. Just after taking the charge of the company he made a quick SWOT (Strength, Weaknesses, Opportunities and Threats) analysis and identified the following areas requiring urgent attention:

- the capital requirements,
- organisational structure,
- technology and marketing,

– industrial relations.

After making familiar himself with the products, technology, organisational structure, people and market, Mr. S.K. Mukherjee initiated a wide range of actions relating to capital requirements, organisational restructuring, technology upgradation, product range, marketing and inducing a sense of motivation. These are described as under:

(a) *Financial Restructuring*

Financial restructuring played a very significant role in turnaround of the company because cash was a major problem. On the finance front, following steps were taken:

1. The company entered into an agreement for the sale of land measuring 15,264 sq. mtrs. at Andheri to Varun Investment, a sister concern of Tata Chemicals and to lease back this land for a period of 45 years at an annual lease rent of Rs. 27.5 lakhs. This decision had brought Rs. 1.36 crores at the time when the company was desperately in need of money.
2. Raised Rs. 3 crores by way of Rights Convertible Bonds. The convertible portion of Rs. 1 crore increased the equity base from Rs. 2.17 crores to Rs. 3.17 crores in 1986. The convertible part of Rs. 100 was compulsorily and automatically converted into one fully paid equity share at par at the end of 12 months. The non-convertible portion of Rs. 200 per bond would be redeemable at par at the end of 7 years from the date of allotment.
3. The three Tata Electric Companies – The Tata Hydro Electric Power Supply Company Limited, The Andhra Valley Power Company Limited and the Tata Power Company Limited — advanced a sum of Rs. 4.5 crores of which Rs. 2,18,19,800 was deposited as an advance towards subscription of additional equity shares through a right issue.
4. During 1987, ICICI in participation with IDBI and IRBI sanctioned a term loan of Rs. 8 crores repayable over a period of eight years starting from 1989. The term loan was given under the Project Finance Participation Scheme in order to finance partly the company's diversification schemes and to

meet the working capital requirements.

5. During November/December 1987, 3,80,000 rights equity shares were issued at Rs. 100 per share of which only 1,26,221 shares were subscribed.
6. Over and above, the company's bankers sanctioned additional working capital facilities to meet the working capital requirements.

(b) *Organisational Restructuring*

Prior to April 1986, the Company had a functional based organisational structure having a high degree of centralisation. Having taken charge of the company in April 1986, Mr. S.K. Mukherjee revamped the organisational structure based on profit centre approach. First, the organisation was divided into three divisions — consumer products, industrial systems, and office automation and computers — based on products followed by decentralisation of authority. Though the process of divisionalisation started in 1979-80, yet could not be effected fully till 1986. These divisions were given complete independence regarding marketing, material, production, personnel, research and development except finance where some sort of unified control exists. Presently they have their own marketing, production, purchase, personnel teams. Even in finance, where some sort of unified control exists, each division has its own finance team. Secondly, the structural changes were followed by the devolution of decision-making power. Three levels of decision making — Head Office, Divisions and Departments — were introduced. S.K. Mukherjee explains 'what can be decided at the division level never comes up to me and what the materials manager can decide he does without going to the divisional head' (*Business World*, April 11-24, 1988). In brief, the concept of total accountability for each division was introduced.

(c) *Focus on Technology*

The company's Research and Development Department was restructured during 1986 creating a separate R & D department for each product division which was centralised for all the products till 1986. To start with, there was no R & D department in NELCO and it was being done by the Tata Electric Companies till 1983. As a consequence, there was about 80 per cent rejection of products because of difficulty in determining whether product design was wrong or the manufacturing was poor. To overcome this problem, the company established its own R & D department in 1980 which started working independently in 1983. Though a considerable investment was made in R & D facilities, equipment and human resources, but lot of time and energy of managers used to be wasted on getting their R & D work done on priority basis because of centralised R & D work. Keeping the above problem in view, a separate R & D department was set-up for each product division in 1986. S.K. Mukherjee says "We are aiming for technical excellence" (*Business World*, April 11-24, 1988).

The focus was laid on to be in the market by design and shifting from a substantial trading base to an in-depth manufacturing base, which was based on technology and marketing. Nelco has collaborated with the various business groups abroad for better and effective integration of R & D activities. These include Mitsubishi Electric and Mita of Japan, *Honeywell*-Bull of Italy, General Electric of the U.S.

(d) *Marketing Thrust*

Prior to April 1986, there was a centralised marketing system for all the products. The same marketing team was selling products ranging from a small set of radio to a industrial electronic system. In 1986, it was restructured having a separate marketing department for each product division — consumer products, industrial systems and office automation. Marketing of products was based on technology and customers requirement. Apart from high-tech ambitions, there was a increased thrust on marketing as indicated in advertising budget which was doubled in 1987 (Rs. 1.51 crores) compared to 1986.

(e) *The People : The Organisation's Strength*

On the industrial relations front, the memo culture was replaced by an open culture in 1986 to instil in the rank and file a sense of motivation. The management started discussing problems of employees across the table whenever they crop up. Efforts were made to have harmonious labour relations. People-oriented strategy was adopted. Management made efforts to charge up the people to fight for a share of market. Participative approach in decision-making was introduced and communicated down to line in a free environment. The decision regarding no induction at the higher level management, no addition to the total, no retrenchment and termination was communicated down to line. It played a crucial role in charging up people to fight for turning around the unit. It inculcated a sense of confidence. Joint Departmental Councils and Joint Plant Councils were constituted. "Workers have proved most cooperative" adds Mukherjee, "In 1986, for instance, there were 300 people idle on the radio side of our operations. We trained them and now they are fully employed else where". Kenny Solomon, Secretary of the NELCO unit of Bombay Labour Union says, "of course there was some initial reluctance. But once we understood that the company's training programmes were going to teach us new skills, we were very keen on them". This could be possible only on account of open culture in discussing the problems of employees. It had a corresponding effect on productivity in terms of sales per worker which increased from Rs. 1.73 lakhs per annum in 1982-83 to Rs. 4.18 lakhs in 1987. Motivated groups and leaders emerged having tremendous intransic energy which proved assets for the organisation.

The strategies discussed above led to the turnaround of NELCO in 1987. The profitability, net working capital, net worth and health score of the company over a period of ten years are shown in Table 5.2 and Table 5.3 respectively. The profile of the company is also given in Table 5.4.

TABLE 5.2: Financial Viability Parameters of National Radio and Electronics Co. Ltd.

(*Rs. in lakhs*)

Year Ending	Net Profit/ Loss	Cash Profit/ Loss	Net Working Capital	Net Worth
March 1980	20	27	66	74
June 1981	–64	–50	–7	10
June 1982	120	146	137	138
June 1983	73	91	94	212
June 1984	90	113	231	326
December 1985	–125	–73	157	464
December 1986	–27	40	429	529
December 1987	74	153	952	720
December 1988	113	195	1236	946
March 1990	45	157	793	1114

TABLE 5.3: Health Score of the National Radio and Electronics Company Limited (NELCO)

(*Multivariate Approach*)

Year	EBIT/TTA@	CF/TTA	CA/CL	NS/TTA	DA/TOE	Health Score*	
						y_1	y_2
1980	.021	.030	1.092	1.209	.396	1.477	1.807
1981	−.031	−.047	.991	1.134	.377	.381	.610
1982	.121	.119	1.148	1.564	.350	3.699	3.375
1983	.094	.054	1.069	1.379	.434	2.859	2.336
1984	.075	.046	1.124	1.275	.474	2.637	2.160
1985	.012	−.013	1.055	1.060	.414	1.199	1.068
1986	.063	.009	1.148	1.243	.397	2.338	1.534
1987	.059	.025	1.245	1.137	.473	1.992	1.734
1988	.077	.025	1.239	1.293	.439	2.674	1.844
1990	.094	.013	1.102	1.185	.465	2.946	1.595

@ EBIT does not include non-operating income/losses since the latter constitutes a major portion of earning before interest and taxes.

* 1. MDA Model for predicting industrial sickness:
y_1 = 19.8927 EBIT/TTA + .0047 CA/CL + .7141 NS/TTA + .4860 DA/TOE
(Yadav, R.A., 'Financial Ratios and The Prediction of Corporate Failure', p.88).

2. MDA Model for appraising the effectiveness of Working Capital Management:
y_2 = 14.5166 CF/TTA + .0015 CA/CL + .8751 NS/TTA + .7914 DA/TOE
(Yadav, R.A., 'Working Capital Management — A Parametric Approach', *The Chartered Accountant*, May 1986).

TABLE 5.4: Profile of the NELCO

Ownership	Private Sector
Age	50 years
Size (No. of employees)	—
Sales	Rs. 5359 lakhs
Products	Electronic Goods
Market	Domestic and Competitive
Technology	Indigenous and Foreign
Apparent Cause of sickness	Mismanagement
Turnaround Period	21 months (April 1986 — December 1987)
Profit prior to Turnaround	Loss of Rs. 1.25 crore in ended December 1985
Profit on Turnaround	Profit of Rs. 73.61 lakhs in ended December 1987
Main Strategy of Turnaround	A happy combination of vision and mission of top management regarding control over cash, setting of targets and chasing them. The vision of the company chairman Ratan Tata. The Mission of the Chief Executive Sh. S.K. Mukherjee.

6

INTERNATIONAL COMPUTERS INDIAN MANUFACTURE LIMITED (ICIM)

International Computers Indian Manufacture Ltd. (ICIM), the country's leading computer company till 1986, suffered a set back in 1987. Sales have grown dramatically over the last four years i.e. from Rs. 24 crores in 1983 to Rs. 45 crores in 1986, but there had not been a commensurate rise in profitability. In an industry growing at the rate of 41 per cent per annum, ICIM's sales slumped from Rs. 46.87 crores in December 1987 to Rs. 36.60 crores in ended March 1989 (24% fall) resulting in a loss of Rs. 5.87 crores. However, in the financial year ended March 1990, ICIM's sales have gone up from Rs. 36.60 crores in 1989 to Rs. 61.54 crores and net profit increased from Rs. 4.70 crores loss in 1989 to Rs. 1.20 crores profit in 1990 (See Table 6.3) Two years ago the company was struggling for its survival, finds a sea change in its performance today and looking for better prospects. All this took less than 18 months. What brought it about?

The Company

Incorporated on 29th March, 1963 at Bombay to manufacture and deal in all kinds of computers, tabulators, accounting and calculating machines and punch cards. It was promoted by International Computers Ltd. (London) having 40 per cent stake in equity and technical collaboration. The company was started with a capital base of Rs. 50 lakhs which has increased to Rs. 579 lakhs in March 1990 (See Table 6.3).

In 1977-78, the company received a letter of intent for the manufacture of 2904 computer systems and started its production during 1979-80. In October 1981, an industrial licence was received for the manufacture of mini computer/micro processor-based systems of the annual capacity of Rs. 2 crores in the company's existing industrial undertaking at Pune. During 1981-82, the company obtained a letter of intent to increase the present licensed capacity for the manufacture of line printers and started its production during 1982-83.

Till 1986, the focus of the company has been on mainframes. Due to sluggish in demand of mainframes and changing Indian computer market, the company planned to improve its main product line and diversify its product range. During 1986 ICIM Quatho Super Micro Computer was introduced. In 1987, Distributed resources system-300, state-of-the art computer was launched. During December 1987, the mainframe series-39 computers based on 5th generation VLS technology incorporating VMC operating machines was introduced. During 1989, the company introduced the PC range and launched Krypton series of machines in association with integrated Micro Products Ltd., U.K. Now the product range of the company covers everything from PCs to mainframes. The company is solidly positioned with a full product range that addresses virtually the whole information technology spectrum.

Key Problems

The company started facing problems in early 1985 on account of instability in management at the top level. The frequent changes in top management did a considerable damage to the performance of the company and its image. Further, the changes at the top took place when the company was passing through a critical time in its operations. The exit of Shri Prem Shivdasani in early 1985 who served a full term as Managing Director was the starting point of management problems in ICIM. Four Chief Executives — Vasant Kher, William Jackson from ICL (UK), Major General Shyam Lal Ghosh and David Beesley ICL UK — had come and gone between early 1985 to November 1988. Though the frequent changes in top management did not result in an exodus of key personnel but generated uncertainty right down the line resulting in overall deterioration in company's performance.

Apart from frequent changes at the top management level, ICIM was faced with several other problems requiring urgent attention. First, ICIM's over dependence on ICL's (London) proprietary technology centring around mainframes reduced it to a mainframe company without adequate market. The Indian Computer market had undergone a radical change and the company could not fall in line with the changing industry standards on account of its excessive dependence on ICL's technology. The computer market in India can best be described as industry standard driven. There were few buyers for the ICIM's non-standard products. Since more than three quarters of India's computer market relates to non-frames products, the company was left high and dry. As a result, the company was able to sell only *two* S-39 mainframes in 1988 (15 month) which was 1.27 per cent of ICIM's installed capacity of 125 computers per annum.

Secondly, launching a number of products as a part of its growth strategy without requisite long-term financial resources was the another mistake on the part of the company. The company introduced a number of products such as mini 101/400 series, the distributed resource system, the line printer and the mainframe series-39. Long- term requisite financial resources were not available to meet the financial requirements of series of products launched. The company had to tap the short-term money market for funds. In 1985 the company raised Rs. 3 crores through inter-corporate deposits at a cost of 17 per cent per annum. So, diversion of short-term funds for long- term uses put the company in liquidity crisis. It was further worsened by the decision of Mr. Ghosh to return Rs. 3 crores borrowed from the inter-corporate deposits market though it was a prudent financial decision. As a result of the financial strategy followed, the company started facing financial crunch.

Thirdly, introducing a series of products and their after sales service resulting in growth of sales led to the problem of higher inventories and bills receivables. As ICIM was selling systems, installation delays was the common phenomenon. So both inventories as well as bills receivables went out of proportion.

Lastly, the company faced problems on the environment front also. With the announcement of New Computer Policy in 1985, the industry moved from a sellers' market to buyers' market. The growth in the market of PCs at an astonishing rate of 200 per cent motivated a large number of companies (146) in this segment alone resulting in fierce competition and price war. The decision of the company to launch PC_2 in early 1986 which was priced 30 per cent higher than the market, was strategically wrong since there was a price war. As a result, the company had to withdraw it from the market after selling only 400 units. Apart from this, the position of the company even in its main product i.e. mainframe segment was also not favourable, since its sole competitor Electronics Corporation of India Ltd. (ECIL) was enjoying a price preference of 15 per cent in the mainframe market. And also the launching of series-39 was delayed by 18 months on account of a stipulation mentioned in the New Computer Policy resulting in loss of market.

The various causes discussed above led to the deterioration of company's position in the computer market and it could sell just two mainframes against its installed capacity of 1125 per annum in 1988 and moreover, there was no sign of recovery. The company was incurring a cash loss of Rs. 40 to Rs. 50 lakhs per month resulting in cash crunch and incurred a net loss of Rs. 5.87 crores during the year ending March 1989.

Key Actions and Results

Keeping in view the deteriorating financial position of the company, International Computers Ltd. (ICL), the U.K.-based company holding 40 per cent stake in equity in ICIM, started searching for a partner having Indian base and can bring requisite financial resources to overcome the immediate problem of liquidity crunch. It was realised by the ICL, the U.K.-based company, that two factors were crucial for the recovery and survival of ICIM : (a) involvement of Indian management in running the company, and (b) diversification of its products range in order to fall in line with industry standards and requisite financial help.

After negotiations, RPG Enterprises signed up a partnership pact with ICIM's London-based company, ICL holding 40 per cent stake in the equity. As per agreement, RPG Enterprises would hold 40 per cent stake in equity in ICIM and run it under the management of a board. As a consequence, Harish Goenka took over the charge of the company as the non-executive Chairman in November 1988. Mr Sumantra Banerjee was appointed as executive head of the company. Banerjee, though a non-computer man, had a fair experience in manufacturing and marketing coupled with a multinational company executive background and technologically aware.

Having taken charge of the company, the new management evaluated the existing position of the company and identified the key areas requiring immediate attention. These were incomplete product range, non-availability of requisite funds, particularly working capital, lack of control over inventory and debtors, under utilisation of capacity, over staffing and low staff morale. It was a mainframes company with no mainframe orders. Hence, the immediate task before the new management was to arrange adequate finance and to take measures to fall in line with the industry standards for the recovery of ICIM. To overcome the problem of liquidity and marketing, various steps were taken both on external and internal front. These were:

(i) RPG Enterprises pumped in sufficient interest free funds i.e., Rs. 3 crores which was later adjusted in a Rs. 5.63 crore convertible debenture issue.

(ii) Keeping in view the nature of the computer market, it was decided to diversify its product range in order to fall in line with the industry standard products i.e. the whole gammut of PCs and minis. Today, its product range covers everything from PCs to mainframes and virtually addresses the whole spectrum of information technology. The most important point to note is that neither of its products is based on ICL known-how, still ICIM's relationship with ICL is as close as it always had been.

(iii) On the internal front, the company was reorganised by divisionalising it into four divisions based on revenue streams — mainframes office systems, maintenance contracts and exports. Since there was an urgent need for top level accountability, the emphasis was laid on accountability on the respective divisional heads which was lacking in the earlier organisational structure. It was realised that introducing new products as per market requirements will be a futile exercise unless the company's organisational structure and operations are streamlined. Marketing division was also restructured keeping in view the market orientation required for selling PCs. The company's sales team was used to the project-oriented selling of mainframes each costing Rs. 1 crore or more requiring time frame of 6-20 months involving long interactive sessions and follow up for materialising a deal. For PCs, sale is to be closed in three to four calls, otherwise it becomes cost ineffective, since margins are low. Since a different market approach was needed, 33 people from the PC sector were recruited, 3 out of 5 regional managers and 7 out of 14 area managers were changed. Efforts were made through intensive crash training programme to inculcate a work culture where marketing managers own and resolve problems without passing the buck. Top priority was given to ensure an immediate 50 per cent growth in sales of all the products. This resulted in increase of sales of all products and as a result the capacity utilisation of factory at Pune went up close to full, which was under-utilised forcing a large part of 324 employees into idleness. The factory could absorb its overhead at a reduced overhead cost per unit. Overhead cost is of particular significance, since testing and quality arrangements are indispensable to meet rigorous international standards in such type of industries.

(iv) Apart from organisational restructuring, various cost cutting measures were also taken to tone up the company's performance and to reduce cost such as rigorous commercial controls over debtors, inventories and borrowings, a focus on short-term perspective by introducing monthly profit and loss account, voluntary retirement scheme, no hiring of air-conditioned cars during outstation tours. 120 people got retirement under the voluntary retirement scheme. The retrenchment of staff under the voluntary retirement scheme was managed effectively. In 1980, ICIM had 1200 people with a turnover of Rs. 11.49 crores. In March 1990, with a staff strength of 875, turnover had touched Rs. 61.54 crores. As a result of the rigorous controls over inventory, bills receivables and borrowings, the stock level declined from Rs. 22 crores to Rs. 14 crores in 12 months' period, debt figures remained static at Rs. 13.5 crores despite a dramatic increase of revenue from Rs. 28 crores (1988) to Rs. 54 crores (1989). Borrowings have come down from Rs. 34 crores to Rs. 24 crores thereby reducing the interest burden from the 1988 average of Rs. 40 lakhs a month to around Rs. 25 lakhs in 1989 (*Business World*, January 17-30, 1990, p. 67).

The strategies discussed above led to the revival of ICIM in the year 1990. The trend analysis of financial parameters indicating the decline and revival of the company is shown in Table 6.1 and Table 6.2. The financial profile of the company over a period of ten years (1980-90) is given in Table 6.3. The profile of the company is also shown in Table 6.4.

TABLE 6.1: Financial Viability Parameters of International Computers Indian Manufacture Ltd.

(Rs. in lakhs)

Year ending	Net profit/ Loss	Cost Profit/ Loss	Net Working Capital	Net Worth
September 1980	76	187	–62	383
September 1981	93	201	–50	437
September 1982	108	225	–47	506
September 1983	82	216	–180	548
September 1984	88	234	–105	596
September 1985	86	267	–70	1024
December 1986	94	250	243	1077
December 1987	38	194	718	1326
March 1989	–587	–329	2250	737
March 1990	120	288	1832	1137

TABLE 6.2: Health Score of International Computers Indian Manufacture Ltd.

(Multivariate Approach)

Year	EBIT/TTA	CF/TTA	CA/CL	NS/TTA	DA/TOE	Health Score*	
						Y_1	Y_2
1980	.126	.085	.925	.835	.261	3.234	2.173
1981	.166	.115	.956	.904	.358	4.120	2.745
1982	.180	.117	.962	1.032	.220	4.429	2.777
1983	.178	.108	.865	1.227	.208	4.522	2.807
1984	.108	.109	.925	1.228	.267	3.106	2.870
1985	.136	.076	.969	1.126	.361	3.689	2.376
1986	.088	.043	1.077	.766	.561	2.575	1.740
1987	.098	.036	1.215	.884	.497	2.828	1.691
1989	–.009	–.063	2.428	.732	.619	.655	.220
1990	.068	.047	1.625	1.013	.499	2.326	1.966

*(1) MDA Model for predicting industrial sickness

Y_1 = 19.8927 EBIT/TTA + .0047 CA/CL + .7141 NS/TTA + .4860 DA/TOE (Yadav, R.A., Financial Ratios and The Prediction of Corporate failure, p. 88)

(2) MDA Model for appraising the effectiveness of Working Capital Management

Y_2 = 14.5166 CF/TTA + .0015 CA/CL + .8751 NS/TTA + .7914 DA/TOE (Yadav, R.A. 'Working Capital Management — A Parametric Approach', *The Chartered Accountant*, May, 1986).

TABLE 6.3: Financial Profile of International Computers of Indian Manufacture Ltd.

(Rs. in lakhs)

Year Ending	September 1980	September 1981	September 1982	September 1983	September 1984	September 1985	(15 months) December 1986	December 1987	(15 months) March 1989	March 1990
Net Sales	1149	1588	1980	2445	2633	3905	4460	4686	4575	6154
Operating Expenses	887	1212	1538	1938	2261	3298	3754	4040	4438	5564
Depreciation	112	108	117	134	146	181	156	156	195	168
Operating Profit	150	268	325	373	226	426	550	490	(−58)	421
Non-operating income/loss	23	23	21	(−18)	134	46	(−35)	29	99	(−9)
Earning before interest and taxes	173	291	346	355	360	472	515	519	41	412
Interest	45	109	142	175	191	288	320	437	628	412
Net profit/Loss	76	94	108	82	88	86	95	38	(−587)	120
Cash profit/Loss	118	202	225	216	234	267	251	194	(−392)	288
Profit retained	40	54	68	42	48	36	54	38	—	120
Equity Capital	250	250	250	250	250	250	250	413	413	579
Net Work	383	437	506	548	596	1024	1077	1327	737	1137
Long term Debt	156	181	172	112	150	159	412	646	2689	2009
Current Liabilities	837	1138	1238	132	1396	2285	3168	3330	1575	2930
Total Tangible Assets	1376	1756	1917	1922	2143	3468	4657	5302	5002	6076
Current Assets	775	1088	1191	1152	1291	2215	3411	4048	3825	4762
Net Working Capital	(−62)	(−50)	(−47)	(−180)	(−105)	(−70)	243	718	2250	1832
Defensive Assets	232	434	339	403	605	1191	1685	2008	2075	2776
Inventory	543	654	852	749	686	1024	1726	2040	1750	1986
Debtors	200	372	308	347	527	1021	1458	1664	1612	2219
Cash and Bank balances	6	5	12	17	23	58	88	126	199	153
Market value per Equity share of Rs 10 High	Rs.21.00	27.00	26.75	30.00	26.00	40.00	40.00	33.00	27.00	35.00
Low	Rs.12.75	15.50	15.00	21.00	22.50	25.00	18.00	16	14.00	30.00

Source: *The Stock Exchange Official Directory*, Bombay.

TABLE 6.4: Profile of ICIM

Ownership	Private Sector
Age	28 years
Size (Number of employees)	930
Sales	Rs 3660 Lakhs
Products	Computers (Main frames, Mini, PCs) and other information Technology products
Market	Domestic and International
Technology	Indigenous and Foreign
Apparent Cause of Sickness (incipient)	Mismanagement (Frequent changes at the top level, and excessive dependence on mainframe products
Turnaround Agency	Business House (RPG Enterprises)
Turnaround Period	18 months (1989-90)
Profitability Prior to Turnaround	Loss of Rs. 5.87 crores in ended March 1990
Profitability on Turnaround	Profit of Rs. 1.20 crores in ended March 1990
Main Strategy of Turnaround	Dedicated efforts of the Dynamic New Chief Executive.

7

SPECIAL STEELS LIMITED (SSL)

The company, which was a sick unit with accumulated losses of Rs. 12.43 crores against an equity capital of Rs. 5.09 crores as on 31 December, 1984, reported a profit of Rs. 6.02 crores during the year ended December 31, 1985. It had been able to wipe out its accumulated losses and build up a handsome reserve of Rs. 21.30 crores as on 31 March, 1989. The company proposed to issue 3,79,650 equity shares of Rs. 100 as bonus shares in the ratio proportion of 1:2 after a gap of 17 years. The capacity utilisation at all the plants had increased resulting in economies of scale. Turnover had increased from Rs. 65 crores in 1984 to Rs. 207 crores in 1989. Since 1985, the company has never looked back, reported profit every year and managed to pay dividend from 1986 onwards. All the plants had achieved more than 100 per cent of the annual rated capacity during the period ended 31 March, 1989. How was this remarkable turnaround of the company achieved in a period of one year?

The Company

Incorporated on 10th May, 1958 as a private company and converted into a Public Limited Company on 28th March, 1961 having its registered office at Borivili (East) in Bombay to manufacture of various types of high carbon wires such as electrode wire, galvanised iron wire, umbrella ribs wire, prestressed concrete wire, rope wire and other wires. The company has the technical collaboration with Felter and Guilleaume Carlswork Eisen and Stake A.G., West Germany for the manufacture of special types of wires and Suzuki Metal Industry Company Ltd., Japan for rendering operational technical assistance to manufacture of sophisticated wires. Apart from the factory at Borivli in Bombay, it has three centres consisting of Bead Wire Plant, Mini Steel Plant and Wire Rod Mill and

Research and Development Centre at Tarapur. The new unit at Tarapur went into production with effect from 1st September, 1976. In July 1979 Gogte Steel Ltd., a sick mini steel plant was merged with the company and resumed its operations with effect from 19th April, 1980.

The company was started with the equity base of Rs. 39 lakhs (39000 shares of Rs. 100 each) in 1958 which has increased to Rs. 759.30 lakhs equity share capital and Rs. 28 lakhs 15 per cent preference shares as on 31st March, 1989 (for details see Table 7.3). The company received a letter of intent for the manufacture of 60,000 tonnes per annum of high carbon and alloy steel wire rods (in size between 5 mm to 13 mm rods in 400 kg minimum coil weight). Industrial licence in this respect was received during 1977-78 with an export commitment of 25 per cent for 5 years. The total cost of this project was estimated at Rs. 888 lakhs. This was to be financed through rights issue of equity capital of Rs. 50 lakhs, loans/debentures of Rs. 710 lakhs and internal accruals of Rs. 128 lakhs. On account of some changes in the process equipment for part of the wire rod mill and inflation, cost of the project increased by Rs. 192 lakhs. The company, therefore, proposed to increase the rights issue of equity shares from Rs. 50 lakhs to Rs. 100 lakhs. The project cost was revised *up-wards* to Rs. 1447 lakhs in 1979-80 due to further delay in the implementation of the project. A further rights issue of Rs. 100 lakhs was proposed to meet the cost overrun. In November 1982, the wire rod mill went into commercial production. During 1988-89, the Government converted the letter of intent to an industrial licence to enhance capacity of wire rod mill to 96000 TPA. Government also endorsed higher capacity of 72000 TPA on billets because of modernisation of main steel plants.

A programme aiming at modernising and reducing costs at the mini steel plant, upgradation of product mix, introduction of new products and replacement of old machines which was drawn up and to be implemented during 1966-68 at a cost of Rs. 67 crores could not take place. Collaboration agreement with a leading Japanese technology suppliers (Suzuki Metal Industry Company Ltd., Japan) was finalised in 1986. Government approval was received for foreign collaboration and import of equipment for modernisation of the mini plant in January 1988. During 1988-89, the company completed the first phase of modernisation of the mini steel plant including introduction of water cooled panels and modern pollution control equipment. The company proposed to set up a cold rolling mill with a 1,00,000 TPA capacity of cold rolled strips and sheets mainly to cater to the requirements of automobile, refrigeration and airconditioning industries as a part of its import substitution programme.

The overall performance of the company was satisfactory till 1979. However, it started deteriorating in 1980 and SSL reported a loss of Rs. 155.5 lakhs for the year ending December 1981. The overall performance of the company continued unsatisfactory for four years till 1984. It had accumulated losses of Rs. 12.43 crores against an equity capital of Rs. 5.09 crore as on 31 December, 1984 (Table 7.3).

Key Problems

The company entered in red on account of lack of industrial culture and unfavourable conditions prevailing in the Steel Wire Industry. There were power cuts ranging from 20 per cent to 50 per cent at Borivili plant with consequent adverse effects on production during the year 1980-81. It faced the problem of demand recession and stiff competition in 1982. The overall performance continued unsatisfactory mainly due to slackness in demand for steel wire products during the year 1983. The workers of the wire rod mill went on strike from 14th May to 14th July, 1984. "SSL was structurally a good company. But the lackadaisical work culture and the non-availability of basic raw materials (i.e. scrap and billets) led to underutilisation of capacity and sickness" says S.A. Sabawala, Chairman SSL and Vice-Chairman of TISCO which owns 51 per cent of its equity" (*Business India,* November 27-December 10, 1989, p. 73). Secondly, the delay in commissioning the wire rod mill at Tarapur that led to the cost-overrun was an added drain on SSL's financial resources. The company started a project of wire rod mill in 1977 at Tarapur, Maharashtra at an estimated cost of Rs. 8.88 crores, which commenced commercial production in 1982 at a cost of Rs. 14.47 crores. Thirdly, the backward integration of Gogte Steels Ltd. (GSL), a sick mini steel plant, in July 1979 and its revival operations also had adverse effect on the financial resources of the company. The GSL was taken over with an objective to produce billets from scrap to be used as raw materials for the Wire Rod Mill so that it can utilise the optimum wire drawing capacity. But, it proved a wrong strategic decision because of demand recession, steep hike in steel prices in wire industry and fierce competition from small scale units in 1980-82. The decision of taking over of GSL was wrongly conceived by the management and consequently proved disastrous for the company.

In brief the company entered into red on account of operational and poorly conceived strategic decisions, lackadaisical work culture, non-availability of basic raw materials (i.e. scrap and billets), under utilisation of capacity and unfavourable conditions prevailing in the steel wire industry.

Key Revival Actions

TISCO Management took over the charge of company with effect from 30th August, 1984, perceiving it a potentially viable unit that could turned around. After analysing and identifying the strengths and weaknesses of the company, Kalmati Investment Company Ltd., a wholly owned subsidiary of TISCO acquired 51 per cent equity capital of SSL and thus making it a subsidiary of TISCO. To start with, TISCO management adopted a strategy of open culture with workers which had a remarkable positive change in production. Workers were disseminated the information and taken into confidence regarding the various problems faced by the unit and its potential viability position. Management entered into an agreement with the workers regarding linkage of wages/salary with productivity and fixation of production norms. Productivity linked scheme of remuneration was introduced. Production norms were fixed. The open culture, productivity — wages linked scheme, fixation of production norms and give and take policy of TISCO was appreciated by the workers. In fact, the TISCO management first thought to close down the Borivli plant which had 1800 workers having a production of less then 3500 tpm. But after continuous rounds of discussion with the workers, the management dropped the idea of closing down and in turn made efforts to create proper work culture which resulted in a remarkable change in production over 6000 tpm. Secondly, the proper control over inventory with a view to ensure the availability of raw materials (billets) was introduced. As a result, the capacity utilisation of wire rod mill improved resulting in reduction of overhead per unit and hence better profit margins. Thirdly, SSL upgraded its product mix. More value added items with better sales realisation were introduced. This strategy was adopted will a view to meet the competition from the small scale units. It concentrated on producing alloy steel wires used in the making of ball bearing and other automobile parts and high carbon wires used for railway sleepers and heavy construction activities.

The new management having open culture with the workers, various motivating schemes, better control over inventory, better capacity utilisation, higher sales realisation and upgraded product mix succeeded to turnaround the unit in 1985, reporting a net profit of Rs. 602.29 lakhs from a net loss of Rs. 562.98 lakhs and Rs. 210.27 lakhs in 1983 and 1984 respectively.

The decline and revival of the company in terms of its financial health parameters – Net profit/loss, Cash profit/loss, Net working capital, Net worth, health score over a period of ten years is shown in Table 7.1 and Table 7.2 respectively. The financial profile over a period of ten years is given in Table 7.3. The profile of the company is also shown in Table 7.4.

The company planned for a modernisation programme to be implemented in two phases in January 1988. The first phase of the programme regarding installation of water cooled panels and modern pollution control equipment has been completed. The second phase of modernisation programme regarding installation of ladle furnace and high power transformer to take care of power problems is yet to be completed. Dacunha, Vice President (Finance), SSL says "The modernisation programme, when completed, will result in higher output, cost reduction, better quality of steel with the consumption of power falling by 150 units per tonne from the present 800 units" (*Business India*, November 27-December 10, 1989, p.77). Now the company has plans for diversification. It has proposed to set up a cold rolling mill with a 1,00,000 tpa of cold rolled strips and sheets mainly to cater to the requirements of automobile, refrigeration, air-conditioning industries. This diversification programme seems very appropriate since it is a part of its import substitution programme. The estimated cost of the project is Rs. 100 crores and it is be commissioned by 1991-92. It would be financed by internal accruals and a right debenture issue. This will result in an import saving of around Rs. 80 crores. The company is also looking into the possibilities of diversification in the area of steel wire for radial tyres.

TABLE 7.1: Financial Viability Parameters of Special Steels Ltd.

(Rs. in lakhs)

Year ending	Net Profit/ Net Loss	Cash Profit/ Loss	Net Working Capital	Net Worth
June 1979	86	155	133	638
June 1980	41	118	−201	421
December 1981	−233	−85	−582	259
December 1982	−322	−221	−910	35
December 1983	−562	−268	−1143	−503
December 1984	−280	9	−857	−707
December 1985	602	892	−716	−6
December 1986	1057	1353	1087	1039
December 1987	795	1128	2071	1665
March 1989	1260	1721	1441	2917

TABLE 7.2: Health Score of Special Steels Ltd.

(Multivariate Approach)

Year	EBIT/ TTA	CF/TTA	CA/CL	NS/TTA	DA/TDE	Health Score*	
						Y_1	Y_2
1979	.134	.072	1.123	1.465	.164	3.797	2.459
1980	.102	.038	.890	1.232	.241	3.029	1.822
1981	0.36	−.013	.787	1.148	.168	1.619	.957
1982	.021	−.046	.664	1.088	.154	1.273	.407
1983	−.005	−.054	.649	1.089	.165	.761	.301
1984	.042	.002	.728	1.335	.149	1.845	1.316
1985	.183	.153	.829	1.842	.181	5.048	3.977
1986	.239	.215	1.386	1.945	.195	6.245	4.980
1987	.191	.164	1.882	1.823	.205	5.218	4.141
1989	.174	.136	1.247	1.632	.255	4.756	3.606

* 1. MDA Model for predicting industrial Sickness:
Y_1 = 19.8927 EBIT/TTA + .0047 CA/CL + .7141 NS/TTA + .4860 DA/TOE (Yadav, R.A. 'Financial Ratios and the Prediction of Corporate Failure' p.88)

2. MDA Model for appraising the effectiveness of working Capital Management
Y_2 = 14.5166 CF/TTA + .0015 CA/CL + .8751 NS/TTA + .7914 DA/TOE (Yadav, R.A. 'Working Capital Management — A Parametric Approach', *The Chartered Accountant*, May 1986).

TABLE 7.3: Financial Profile of Special Steels Ltd.

(Rs. in lakhs)

	Ending June 1979	June 80	(18 months) Dec. 81	Dec. 82	Dec. 83	Dec. 84	Dec. 85	Dec. 86	Dec. 87	(15 months) March 89
Net Sales	3144	3753	7766	5133	5360	6507	10734	12224	12509	20603
Operating Expenses	2816	3383	7423	4958	5156	6037	9432	10475	10943	17997
Depreciation	69	77	148	101	294	289	290	296	333	461
Operating Profit	259	293	195	74	(−90)	181	1012	1453	1233	2145
Non-operating income/ loss	29	17	48	24	46	23	56	49	79	53
Earning before interest and taxes	288	310	243	98	(−24)	204	1068	1502	1312	2198
Interest	183	269	475	420	538	485	466	445	376	473
Net Profit/Loss	86	41	(−232)	(−322)	(−562)	(−280)	602	1057	795	1260
Cash Profit/Loss	155	118	(−85)	(−221)	(−268)	9	892	1353	1128	1721
Profit Retained	47	7	(−233)	(−322)	(−562)	(−280)	602	894	669	1062
Equity Capital	300	300	350	409	509	509	609	759	759	759
Pref. Capital	83	83	83	111	111	111	111	111	68	28
Net Worth	638	421	259	35	(−503)	(−707)	(−6)	1039	1665	2917
Long-term Debts	431	801	1516	1965	2165	2423	1643	2425	2847	1358
Current liabilities	1077	1828	2732	2715	3258	3155	4189	2819	2348	5825
Total Tangible Assets	2146	3050	4508	4716	4920	4871	5827	6283	6860	10101
Current Assets	1210	1627	2150	1805	2115	2298	3473	3906	4419	7266
Defensive Assets	464	816	832	766	852	901	1703	2041	2246	3669
Net Working Capital	133	(−201)	(−582)	(−910)	(−1143)	(−857)	(−716)	1087	2071	1441
Inventories	746	811	1318	1039	1263	1397	1770	1865	2173	3597
Debtors	261	478	518	536	626	661	1405	1708	1664	2522
Cash and Bank Balances	26	52	130	133	129	139	214	219	264	239

Source: The Stock Exchange Official Directory, Bombay.

TABLE 7.3 A: Market Value of Equity Shares

(Rs. 100 per share)

Year	High	Low
1979	121	97
1980	105	98
1981	126.25	102.50
1982	105	58
1983	90	60
1984	117.50	66
1985	340	112
1986	320	250
1987	780	270
1988	825	575
Mar 1989	1400	1160

Source: The Stock Exchange Official Directory, Bombay.

TABLE 7.4: Profile of Special Steels Ltd.

Ownership	Private Sector
Turnaround Agency	TATA Management — TISCO
Age	32 years
Size (No. of Employees)	1800
Sales	Rs. 6507 lakhs
Products	High Carbon Steel wires, Steel Wire Rods
Market	Domestic
Technology	Indigenous and Foreign
Apparent Cause of Sickness	Lack of Industrial culture and Demand recession, unfavourable conditions in the Steel Wire Industry.
Turnaround Period	1984-85
Profitability Prior to turnaround	Accumulated losses of Rs. 1243 lakhs as on 31st Dec. 1984. Losses during three preceding years - Rs. 322 lakhs, Rs. 562 lakhs, 280.27 lakhs during the year 1982, 1983, 1984 respectively
Profitability on Turnaround	Net Profit of Rs. 602 lakhs during the year ended December 1985.
Main Strategy of Turnaround	– Change in Top management – Creating Proper work culture – Productivity-linked wage scheme – Change in product-mix.

8

KAMANI TUBES LIMITED (KTL)

The Kamani Tubes Ltd. stopped production and ceased working in August 1985. The company incurred a loss of Rs. 108 lakhs in the year ending December 1984 and the workers had not been paid wages from December 1984 till the stoppage of work in August 1985 and the employees contribution to provident fund amounting to Rs. 3.5 lakhs was not deposited with the provident fund authorities. The accumulated losses were Rs. 283 lakhs as on 31st December, 1984. However the company was taken over by the Employees Cooperative Society as per the decision of the Supreme Court as on 19 September, 1988 that turned the corner resulting in a net operating profit of Rs. 78 lakhs during the year ending March 1990 (See Table 8.2). How was this revival of the company accomplished?

The Company

Established in 1960 in Bombay, the company pioneered the manufacture of non-ferrous tubes in India. In its hey-days, the company accounted for almost 60 per cent of the total domestic output of non-ferrous tubes and supplied it to a number of industries such as power generation, defence, oil refining, sugar, fertilisers, ship-building, automobiles, light electricals and air-conditioning. It was the sole manufacturer of primer tubes used in weapons production. The company flourished in the first 12 years of its existence, achieving a turnover of Rs. 4.93 crores and profit before tax of Rs. 71.77 lakhs in 1972. But by 1975, despite of increase in its turnover to Rs. 5.92 crores, the company began to suffer losses. Over the next decade, the company's accumulated losses kept on mounting despite the increase in turnover (Rs. 6.22 crores in 1982). The company had to suspend its operations in September 1985, it could not secure working capital funds from the banks. Kamani Tubes accumulated losses were Rs. 4.42 crores as against its paid-up capital and reserves of Rs. 97 lakhs as on 31st December, 1985.

The Key Problems

As in majority of the sick industrial unit cases (RBI, Srivastava and Yadav), the decline and ultimate closure of the Kamani Tubes has also been attributed principally to mismanagement.

As early as 1976, the Kamani Employees Union (KEU) had drawn the attention of the Government to management practices in KTL that were detrimental to the company. It was alleged that the Kamani's were systematically siphoning funds from the company by overinvoicing purchases, undermoving bills, appointing unofficial dealers, selling high quality material as substandard and making exaggerated claims of metal burning losses. Initially these allegations were ignored. However, later on both banks and financial institutions found the above as the most probable causes for the failure of the company.

The problem of mismanagement of the company was further aggravated by the internal discord of the Kamani's family over the assets of the Kamani group which started just after the death of Shri Ramji Bhai Kamani, the founder of KTL – in the early eighties. The Kamani family's discord over the group's assets gave rise to disputes and litigation ultimately culminating in law suits where all the concerned members of the family were impleaded. The company was faced with a winding up position filed by a family member who was removed from its Board. Disputes and litigation made the bankers and financial institutions skeptical about credibility of the company. As a consequence of this, KTL could not secure a term loan that it had been negotiating for a major capital investment programme. Moreover credit facilities were suspended by its principal bankers – Bank of India and Canara Bank. However the minimum credit facilities were restored by Canara Bank on a request by the State Government to keep the company survive. The interest liability of company to bankers accumulated to Rs. 5 crores besides the unpaid wages to its 700 workers and other statutory dues amounting to Rs. 2 crores.

In the course of proceedings, Supreme Court impressed on the various groups of Kamani's family the need for speedily resolving the disputes so that neither the units nor the workers employed are ruined. Keeping this in view, in April 1984 Supreme Court appointed a retired judge A.C. Gupta as mediator to resolve disputes and innumerable problems faced by the company. The case of KTL, which stopped its working in August 1985, was also referred to justice A.C. Gupta. When the case of KTL came, he noted in his report of December 1986, 'The parties present agreed that whether ultimately 90 per cent shares of the company were to be sold or the factory was to be run by the Kamani's, it was essential that some competent person should be appointed without delay to protect the interests of the company in the meantime'. Accordingly, D.H. Nanavati, a solicitor, was appointed to take the charge of the company's books, represent it in litigation, collect all outstandings owed to it and negotiate with the company's creditors and workers regarding the settlement of their dues. More important point to be noted was that all the parties were behaving in the whole exercise in such a way as if all possibilities of reviving KTL have been exhausted. In such circumstances, the only alternative left was to find an entrepreneur or some other company to take over KTL. At that time, KEU expressed its desire to take over the management of the sick unit with the intention to revive it. In the light of the above developments, justice A.C. Gupta directed the different groups of the Kamani family to find a buyer who can purchase 91 per cent shares held by them and agree to negotiate with the workers for their dues within a period of six weeks and permitted the KEU also to formulate a revival scheme for the rehabilitation of KTL.

The Kamani's, banks and the State Government could not find buyer for the 91 per cent share held by the Kamani's in KTL despite their sustained efforts. In the meantime, the KEU submitted a comprehensive proposal for the takeover and revival of the sick Kamani Tubes by a cooperative society with KTL employees as its members. The society enrolled 641 employees as its members out of total 741. The objectives of society were also mentioned in clear terms.

The revival scheme submitted by the workers was referred to BIFR by the Supreme Court on 30 October, 1987 with a direction to assests its viability and file a feasibility report. BIFR, in turn directed Bank of India to furnish details of the scheme in consultation with the workers and appointed IDBI as an operating agency. IDBI was asked to evaluate the viability of the proposed revival scheme and to examine in depth the proposed organisational set up of KTL, current prices and cost structure, projected demand and cash flow and past performance of similar companies. BIFR submitted its feasibility report on revival scheme prepared by the workers and modified by

IDBI to the Supreme Court in January 1988 for its consideration.

The revival scheme submitted by the Kamani family on 12 September, 1988 was also considered by the Supreme Court before delivering its judgment in favour of workers. The revival package prepared Kamani's was rejected by the Court since there was no firm commitment of funds by Kamani's, financial institutions and bankers.

The Supreme Court approved the workers' scheme as sanctioned by BIFR and delivered its judgment on 19 September, 1988 in favour of KTL employees. The Court allowed the workers to take over the company's equity from the Kamani family and restart production.

Rehabilitation Scheme as approved by BIFR

The Board for Industrial and Financial Reconstruction approved the KEU scheme for the revival of KTL whose 700 odd workers were on the verge of starvation because of not getting their wages for the past over three years. The BIFR considered the various objections raised by the members of the rival groups of the Kamani family and the Indian Non-Ferrous Metals Manufacturers Association. It pointed out that the revival of KTL would help to sustain as many as 600 workers who are virtually starving without getting wages for the last three years. While upholding the KTL Employees Cooperative Society Scheme, the BIFR said 'the factors of the economy of the area, revenue loss to the governments and large funds already at stake also cannot be ignored'. The salient features of the revival scheme approved by the BIFR are as under:

1. *Change in Management*

The ownership and management of KTL would be transferred to workers cooperative – The Kamani Tubes Limited Sahakari Society (KTLSS). The management of KTL shall be vested in reconstituted Board of Directors consisting of professionally qualified and experienced persons. The reconstructed Board of Directors would comprise two nominees of State Government, two professional Directors having expertise in the related fields, one Director nominee of the banks, one nominee of financial institutions and at least two nominees of the workers cooperative society. It would be responsible for overall direction and policies of KTL.

A Management Committee would also be set up to look after the day to day working of the company. It will meet more frequently than the Board for timely disposal of issues requiring management decisions. The running of the company will be monitored by an Implementation Committee with nominees from the IDBI, the BIFR, the State Government banks and KTL. This Committee will work in close coordination with the Board of Directors of KTL.

2. The Workers' Cooperative – the Kamani Tubes Ltd. Sahakari Society (KTLSS) will take over the existing share capital of KTL (Rs. 96 lakhs) at a price of Re. 1 per share. The decision of transferring the share capital of KTL held by Kamani's (Rs. 96 lakhs) to workers cooperative at a reduced value of Rs. 9.6 lakhs was taken since the Kamani's were responsible for the debacle of the company and net worth was negative.

3. To increase the equity base of the company, both the workers cooperative society and the Maharashtra Government will contribute Rs. 1.40 crore equally to the equity capital. The workers will contribute Rs. 12,000 each which will be raised from their provident fund Rs. 2,000 each and loan of Rs. 10,000 each from the Urban Cooperative Banks.

4. IDBI would provide a loan of Rs. 50 lakhs against working capital margin. Out of the funds contributed by the workers, State Government and IDBI, Rs. 60 lakhs would be spent towards start up expenses and the balance for raising need based working capital.

5. *Workers' Commitments*

The workers agreed to wage freeze for next three years, deferment of annual increments for initial two years and reduction in payment of wages. They also agreed to forego their dues after December 12, 1985 till commissioning of the plant. The outstanding of Rs. 2 crores payable to the employees as on 12 December, 1985 would be effective after other dues standing against the KTL are cleared.

6. *Government and Banks Assistance*

The Government of Maharashtra agreed for declaring KTL as a relief undertaking, deferment of penalty on arrears of sales tax, deferment of current taxes of Rs. 88 lakhs. Financial institutions and banks agreed to liberalise the recovery of outstanding dues till KTL starts production in full swing. Working capital would be made available at a concessional interest rate of 13.5 per cent per annum. However, Urban Cooperative Banks could not provide funds to workers and therefore IDBI came forward and provided Rs. 60 lakhs to help workers to buy shares.

7. The surplus real estate of KTL will be sold realising an estimated amount of Rs. 350 lakhs to meet the shortage of funds.

8. The production was estimated to be 1200 tonnes of rods and 960 tonnes of tubes in the first year. By the third year, it would go up to 1350 tonnes of rods and 1200 tonnes of tubes. These estimates were made keeping in view the state of plant and machinery. The estimated production, sales and profitability for three years is given in Table 8.1.

TABLE 8.1: Projected Production, Sales and Profitability Over a Period of Three Years

Production	Year 1	Year 2	Year 3
	Tonnes	Tonnes	Tonnes
Roads	1200	1350	1350
Tubes	960	1140	1200
	Rs. in lakhs	Rs. in lakhs	Rs. in lakhs
Sales	1595	1871	1955
Gross Profit	123	157	'162
Interest	32	51	53
Depreciation	9	9	9
PBT	82	97	100

The shortage of funds if arises could be met by sale of surplus real estate of Rs. 350 lakhs.

9. The workers agreed for a ban on strike or go slow tactics in the KTL for three years, fixation of production norms, linking of wages with such norms, observing strict discipline by stoppage of absenteeism and overtime and the enforcement of management's right for transfer of employees.

Key Results

The ownership and management of Kamani Tubes Limited was effectively changed into the hands of workers cooperative society. The Board of Directors was reconstituted as per the revival scheme approved by the BIFR. The Management Committee; and implementation Committee have also been set up. The overhaul of plant and machinery was undertaken and completed at a cost of Rs. 60 lakhs. Funds were raised as per revival scheme except the workers subscription (apart from Rs. 9.6 lakhs) towards equity, where they could raise only Rs. 11 lakhs out of Provident Fund. They could not get funds from Urban Cooperative Bank. IDBI came to rescue and subscribed Rs. 60 lakhs, towards share capital of the company to be repurchased by workers cooperative society over a period of six years. KTL started deduction at 10 per cent of salary towards it. The Kamani Tubes Limited had started its production in April 1989. KTL had a operating profit of Rs. 78 lakhs during the year ending March 1990 despite low level of production in the initial month of April because of closure of about 4 years, staff competition in the market from small scale sector, reduction in selling prices of copper tubes to the extent of 20 per cent by its cometitors.

The operational performance of the company for the period April 1989 to March 1990 and the financial profile of the company from 1974 to 1984 are given in Table 8.2 and Table 8.3 respectively. The financial viability parameters – Net profit/loss, cash profit/loss, net working capital, net worth and health score over a period of ten years (1975-1984) are shown in Table 8.4 and Table 8.5, the profile of the company is also given in Table 8.6.

TABLE 8.2: Operational Performance of Kamani Tubes Limited for the year April 1989 to March 1990

(Rs. in Lakhs)

Sales	1030
Less Excise & Sales Tax	166
Net Sales	864
Operating Cost	780
Depreciation	6
Operating Profit	78
Non-Operating Income	9
Non-Operating Expenses	10
Earning before Interest and Taxes	77
Interest	44
Net Profit	33
Net Cash Profit	39

TABLE 8.3: Financial Profile of Kamani Tubes Ltd.

(Rs. in lakhs)

	Year ending December									
	1975	1976	1977	1978	1979	1980	1981	1982	1983	1984
Net Sales	572	553	551	556	514	200	349	575	495	479
Operating Expenses	570	542	538	576	531	298	412	614	502	557
Depreciation	9	10	10	10	10	10	10	10	11	9
Operating Profit	(−7)	1	3	(−30)	(−27)	(−108)	(−73)	(−49)	(−18)	(−87)
Non Operating Income/loss	43	57	55	57	58	67	36	128	66	31
Earning before Interest and Taxes	36	58	58	27	31	(−41)	(−37)	79	48	(−56)
Interest	60	55	58	60	54	54	52	51	46	52
Net Profit/Loss	(−34)	3	00	(−33)	(−23)	(−95)	(−89)	28	2	(−109)
Cash Profit/Loss	(−25)	13	10	(−23)	(−13)	(−85)	(−79)	38	12	(−100)
Equity capital	96	96	96	96	96	96	96	96	96	96
Net Worth	124	127	126	98	75	(−20)	(−109)	(−80)	(−80)	(−186)
Long Term Debt	278	316	297	307	320	316	376	387	361	448
Current Liabilities	216	194	238	200	159	198	240	239	228	254
Total Tangible Assets	618	637	661	605	554	494	507	546	509	516
Current Assets	447	471	503	455	412	363	385	444	418	434
Defensive Assets	214	247	261	240	275	270	280	309	282	304
Net Working Capital	231	277	265	255	253	165	145	205	190	180
Inventories	233	224	242	215	137	93	105	135	136	130
Debtors	85	109	131	79	96	68	74	92	73	70
Cash & Bank Balances	4	3	4	9	12	6	8	33	13	5
Loans and Advances	125	135	126	152	167	196	198	184	196	229

Source: The Stock Exchange Official Directory, Bombay.

TABLE 8.4: Financial Viability Parameters Kamani Tubes Ltd.

(Rs. in lakhs)

Year	Net Profit/ Loss	Cash Profit/ Loss	Net Working Capital	Net Worth
1975	−34	−25	231	124
1976	3	13	277	127
1977	00	10	265	126
1978	−33	−23	255	98
1979	−23	−13	253	75
1980	−95	−85	165	−20
1981	−89	−79	145	−109
1982	28	38	205	−80
1983	2	12	190	−80
1984	−109	−100	180	−186
April 1989- March 1990	33	39	NA	NA

TABLE 8.5: Health Score of Kamani Tubes Limited

(Multivariate Approach)

Year	EBIT/@ TTA	CF/TTA	CA/CL	NS/TTA	DA/TDE	Health Score*	
						Y_1	Y_2
1975	.011	−.041	2.069	.925	.375	.633	.513
1976	.01	.018	2.427	.868	.454	.870	1.384
1977	.004	.015	2.113	.833	.485	.918	1.334
1978	.049	−.038	2.275	.919	.416	−.106	.585
1979	−.048	−.023	2.591	.928	.517	−.029	.891
1980	−.218	−.172	1.833	.405	.906	−3.598	−1.423
1981	−.144	−.156	1.604	.688	.679	−2.036	−1.123
1982	−.089	.069	1.857	1.053	.503	−.765	2.324
1983	.035	.024	1.833	.972	.561	.279	1.646
1984	−.168	−.194	1.708	.922	.546	−2.440	−1.575

* 1. MDA Model for predicting industrial sickness
Y_1 = 19.9827 EBIT/TTA + .0047 CA/CL + .7141 NS/TTA + .4860 DA/TOE
(Yadav, 1986. p.88)

2. MDA model for appraising the effectiveness of working capital management
Y_2 = 14.5166 CF/TTA + .0015 CA/CL + .8751 NS/TTA + .7914 DA/TOE
(Yadav, *The Chartered Accountant*, May 1986)

@ EBIT does not include non operating income/los since the latter constitutes a major portion of earning before interest and taxes.

TABLE 8.6: Profile of Kamani Tubes Limited

Ownership	Private Sector
Age	25 years
Size (Number of Employees)	700
Sales	Rs. 479 lakhs
Products	Non-Ferrous Tubes
Market	Domestic
Apparent cause of Sickness	Mismanagement
Turnaround Agency	The workers cooperative — The Kamani Tubes Limited Sahakari Society
Turnaround Period	April 1989-March 1990
Profitability Prior to Turnaround	Net loss of Rs. 109 lakhs during the year ended December 1984
Profitability on Turnaround	Operating Profit of Rs. 78 lakhs in ended March 1990
Main Strategy of Turnaround	Change in Top Management, Financial Restructuring, Dedicated Efforts of KTL Employees

9

ANGLO FRENCH TEXTILES LIMITED (AFT)

Spreaded over 56 acres land, sustaining about 7000 workers, AFT, the 90 years old mill was closed down on 4th July, 1983. Efforts were made at various levels for two and a half years to revive AFT, but could not succeed. Expert bodies had expressed serious doubts when the Government of India agreed on nationalisation of the unit and set up the Pondicherry Textile Corporation to bring AFT under its umbrella in 1985. It had accumulated losses of Rs. 198.55 lakhs, negative working capital of Rs. 337.48 lakhs and negative net worth of Rs. 21.59 lakhs as on 31st December, 1982 (see Table 9.3). Despite this, it was nationalised and handed over to Pondicherry Textile Corporation in December 1985 for revival. P.M. Nair was appointed as Chairman and Managing Director of the company. He turned the corner in six months against the experts, estimate of one year. He took over the charge of the company in December 1985 as an executive head and got it started working on 10th June, 1986. AFT reported a turnover of Rs. 16 crores making a profit of Rs. 123 lakhs in the first year and turnover of Rs. 31 crores with a profit of Rs. 42.64 lakhs in the second year (1987-88).

How was this miracle of turnaround accomplished ?

Background of the Company

AFT was incorporated in England in 1898 and established a cotton textile mill known as Rodier Mills in Pondicherry in the very same year to manufacture cotton textile goods—long cloth, *dhoties, sarees, sheetings, plain shirtings*. The mill at Pondicherry was equipped with 44256 spindles, 1055 looms and ancillary equipment including a power plant and dyeing and bleaching unit when it was transferred to

Indian Union in 1951. It was managed by Best and Co. Pvt. Ltd., as managing agents till 1963. Prior to its transfer to Indian Union, almost the entire products of Pondicherry Cotton Textile Mills used to be exported to French markets. After that it started facing problems in overseas markets which necessitated for the company to find new markets. The persistent efforts of the management to have its marketing network in India had the desired results. And by the end of 1958, it had normal business.

A comprehensive modernisation scheme was taken up in 1959 and completed by the end of 1963. The management of the company was taken over by C.S. Ramachary, a known industrialist in textile industry, in 1963. The company flourished and was known for its quality products in the international market under the Ramachary management. It used to export 75 per cent of its products to France, Belgium, U.K., West Germany, Italy, Netherlands and United States.

In 1964, the company secured a letter of intent for an expansion of its capacity by 25000 spindles and 400 Picanol automative looms. It commissioned a new mill in 1970 at a total cost of Rs. 2.37 crores. As a result of starting a new mill, the production and sales were increased resulting in higher profitability. In 1973, the company took up a convas mill project involving the installation of 12400 spindles and 72 heavy duty looms at an estimated cost of Rs. 4.01 crores. It started its operations in 1975-76. Subsequently, a modernisation scheme was implemented in 1976. IDBI sanctioned a soft loan of Rs. 75 lakhs for the renovation and modernisation of the mill.

The company was started with a share capital of Rs. 48 lakhs (Rs. 30 lakhs equity shares and 18 lakhs 6 per cent preference shares) in 1951 which increased to Rs. 99 lakhs (Rs. 81 lakhs equity shares and Rs. 18 lakhs 9.5 per cent preference shares) in 1982. The capital structure of the company is shown in Table 9.3.

In July 1981, the management of the company was taken over by Somani Group who acquired 52 per cent equity of the company. Though the performance of company was not satisfactory even before taking the charge of management by Somani Group, it got aggravated. The financial position deteriorated very fast subsequently. This culminated in the closure of the mill on 4th July, 1983 under the management of Somani Group.

Key Problems

The deteriorating performance of the company and ultimately its closure from July 4, 1983 may be attributed to the following factors:

- Mismanagement of the company particularly by Somani Group.
- Siphoning of funds by the management.
- Labour problems—strikes, go slow tactics, long absenteeism, destructive attitude of trade unions.
- Recession in demand, particularly in the foreign markets.
- Power cuts
- Obsolete plant and machinery in all the three units of the mill—spinning, weaving and composite
- Not falling in line with industry norms because of poor product-mix, preponderance of grey cotton and narrow width looms producing varieties not easily saleable in the market
- High turnover (exodus) of trained and skilled workers in 1981.

Revival Actions

After two and a half years revival efforts made at various levels, AFT was taken over by the Government and handed over to Pondicherry Textile Corporation (PTC) for its revival in December 1985. PTC was established specifically to revive Anglo French Textiles Ltd. which was being considered a gone case even by the experts. PTC handed over the management to P.M. Nair who was appointed as Chairman and Managing Director of the company. Nair accepted the task with determination but laid down the condition of complete functional autonomy with no political interference in internal affairs of the company which was agreed in words and actions by the government. "I must admit they stuck to their words", Nair says (*Business World* February 28-March 13, 1990).

Having taking charge of the company as an executive head, he set up a task force with an action plan and made an open appeal to the workers to come and talk directly to the management and rejoin the organisation. He was firm not to deal with the workers through unions (26 unions) which were very active and allegedly responsible for the closure of the mill. Actually it was testing time for the new management. He did not yield to the pressure of unions. Ultimately his open appeal to the workers had positive effect and a list of workers willing to rejoin the unit was prepared. It was considered to be a significant achievement of the new management towards the revival of the unit, since workers were scared to report on account of active unions. It opened the channel of communication that helped in building up a culture of free and frank discussion. As a result of this, today no union is operating within the mill and all decisions are being taken in consultation with the workers directly.

Apart from having the workers rejoined, a wide range of actions were taken. These were:

1. All assets were taken over by the new management without any liability. A special allocation of Rs. 12 crores was made by the Government towards making payment of Rs. 7.65 crores to the previous management by way of compensation and the balance to meet the initial expenses relating to revival of the unit.
2. Plants and machinery as well as the auxiliary equipments were in dilapidated condition. To put them back in working order, an approach of getting it done by the existing staff engineers and workmen was adopted instead of contracting it outside. Even civil engineering jobs like rebuilding of water tanks etc. were also performed by the staff. This had resulted in slashing the revamping time and cost. The rehabilitation of convas mill of AFT was completed in one and a half month at a cost of Rs. 4 lakhs against an estimated cost of Rs. 14 lakhs by the experts. All the three units of AFT — spinning, weaving and composite—were overhauled and put back in working shape by incurring only Rs. 54 lakhs.
3. As many as 1155 workers were retrenched as a part of cost cutting measures.
4. Product mix was diversified to include more profitable and marketable products. These include more processed cloth because of more value addition and wider width sheetings to meet the changed market requirements.
5. It decided to produce cloth beyond the width produced by Bombay Dyeing and Mafatlal, the widest cloth sheet in the country. Keeping the above in view it imported 230 Russian

projectile looms at a cost of around Rs. 12 crores under the Indo-USSR bilateral protocol. A wide width stentor was developed in collaboration with SLM Maneklal. It was the only of its kind in the country. Today beyond 90 inches wide sheeting is the expertise of AFT.

6. Rigorous quality control was exercised. As a result today AFT has quality products and hence significant domestic and export market. "AFT's quality is as good as that of Century's, the market leader. In other words, it is top quality," says M.M. Ratham, Executive Director, Cotton Textiles Export Promotion Council (*Business World*, February 28-March 13, 1990).
7. On the front of motivation and desciplining of workers, various schemes were introduced. These include 24 hours dispensary for workers and their families, making available the best medicine, supply of meal at the canteen round the clock at a subsidised rate i.e. Rs. 2 per meal, converting a part of the mill compound into a vegetable garden, a welfare fund with matching contribution by workers and management, a death relief fund with the contribution by each worker, an open door approach in discussing and settling issues, introducing a new work ethic and an uniform in blue for everyone including the Chairman, seven working days instead of six and rationalisation of workforce. Productivity delivery schedules were strictly adhered to. The various schemes mentioned above motivated the workers resulting in their increased involvement in work. The disciplinary measures were accepted by the workers.

A wide range of actions initiated by the motivated and determined top management with no political interference led to the revival of AFT within a period of six months against the experts' estimate of one year. Table 9.3 indicates the financial profile of the company over a period of ten years. Financial parameters — Net profit/loss, Cash profit/loss, Net working capital, Net worth and health score of the company over a period of ten years are shown in Tables 9.1 and 9.2 respectively. The profile of the company is also given in Table 9.4.

TABLE 9.1: **Financial Viability Parameters of Anglo French Textiles Ltd.**

(*Rs. in lakhs*)

Year ending December	Net profit/loss	Cash profit/loss	Net working capital	Net worth
1974	15	71	23	251
1975	4	61	12	248
1967	26	91	19	264
1977	−132	−76	−123	132
1978	−25	35	−153	122
1979	86	126	−41	196
1980	40	79	29	227
1981	−126	−78	−194	137
1982	−159	−117	−337	−22

TABLE 9.2: Health Score of Anglo French Textiles Limited

(*Multivariate Approach*)

Year	EBIT/TTA	CF/TTA	CA/CL	NS/TTA	DA/TOE	Health Score* y_1	y_2
1974	.078	.072	1.040	1.660	.082	2.782	2.564
1975	−.013	.061	1.019	1.812	.133	1.105	2.578
1976	.087	.075	1.024	1.772	.135	3.066	2.748
1977	−.046	−.065	.873	1.919	.106	0.511	0.821
1978	.056	.020	.823	2.037	.113	2.627	2.164
1979	.168	.125	.948	2.072	.134	4.891	3.735
1980	.105	.069	1.034	2.311	.115	3.800	3.117
1981	−.162	−.063	.812	2.077	.084	−1.695	0.971
1982	−.016	−.108	.675	2.542	.088	1.243	.727

* (1) MDA Model for predicting industrial sickness
y_1 = 19.8927 EBIT/TTA + .0047 CA/CL + .7141 NS/TTA + .4860 DA/TOE
(Yadav, R.A., 1986, p.88).

(2) MDA Model for appraising the effectiveness of Working Capital Management
y_2 = 14.5166 CF/TTA + .0015 CA/CL + .8751 NS/TTA + .7914 DA/TOE
(Yadav, R.A., *The Chartered Accountant*, May 1986).

TABLE 9.3: Financial Profile of Anglo-French Textiles Ltd.

(*Rs. in lakhs*)

		Year Ending December								
		1974	1975	1976	1977	1978	1979	1980	1981	1982
Sales		1617	1803	2139	2248	2235	2076	2632	2591	2738
Operating Expenses		1485	1759	1968	2246	2126	1868	2473	2745	2712
Depreciation		56	57	65	56	47	39	39	48	43
Operating Profit		76	—	106	(−54)	62	169	120	(−202)	(−17)
Non-operating Profit/Loss		1	96	—	20	16	13	17	203	18
Earnings before Interest and Taxes		75	82	106	(−36)	78	181	137	01	01
Interest		61	78	80	96	103	95	97	127	160
Net Profit/Loss		14	4	26	(132)	(−250)	86	40	(126)	(159)
Cash Profit/Loss		70	61	91	(−76)	22	126	79	(−78)	(−117)
Profit Retained		11	(−2)	17	(−132)	(12)	75	31	(126)	(159)
Equity Capital		45	45	45	45	45	45	45	80	81
Net Worth		251	248	264	132	122	196	227	137	(22)
Long Term Debt		151	119	137	71	19	10	53	75	59
Current Liabilities		572	628	806	973	866	796	858	1035	1038
Total Tangible Assets		974	995	1207	1171	1097	1002	1139	1247	1077
Current Assets		595	640	825	850	713	755	887	841	701
Defensive Assets		122	235	265	238	241	250	286	231	239
Net Working Capital		123	12	19	(−123)	(−153)	(−41)	29	(−194)	(−337)
Inventories		473	405	560	612	472	505	601	610	462
Debtors		106	140	184	188	219	187	192	175	186
Cash & Bank Balances		1	14	11	7	20	12	55	40	20
Market Price per Equity Shares of Rs. 100	High (Rs.)	290	235	226	263	205	197	225	220	122
	Low (Rs.)	194	175	214	213	170	170	166	124	102

Source: The Stock Exchange Official Directory, Bombay.

TABLE 9.4: Profile of the Anglo French Textiles Ltd.

Ownership	Private Sector (Presently in Public Sector)
Turnaround Agency	Regulating Authority during Turnaround Pondicherry Textile Corporation (PTC)
Age	92 years
Size (No. of Employees)	5399 Workers
Sales	Rs. 2737 lakhs
Products	Textiles
Market	Domestic and International
Technology	Indigenous and Foreign
Apparent Cause of Sickness	Mismanagement and labour unrest
Turnaround Period	1986-87
Profitability Prior to Turnaround	Net loss of Rs. 159 lakhs during ending December 1982
Profitability on Turnaround	Profit of Rs. 123 lakhs during 1986-87
Main Strategy of Turnaround	Aggressive and Dynamic Chief Executive and Management Team

10

KUMARDHUBI ENGINEERING WORKS LIMITED (KEW)*

Kumardhubi Engineering Works Limited (KEW) was incorporated in 1915, having its registered office in Calcutta and factory at Kumardhubi, Bihar, to manufacture of steel castings and forgings, steel billets, other products of iron and steel, mobile cranes and undertaking construction of ropeway and other structural engineering works for railways, government and local bodies and commercial concerns. It was started with a paid-up capital of Rs. 27 lakhs. The financial profile of the company for ten years is given in Table 10.1. The profile of financial viability parameters and health score is shown in Tables 10.2 and 10.3. The company, which had its name in steel castings and rerolling of special sections, closed its operations totally in 1979 which remained for next five years.

In August 1984, it was taken over by the TISCO management. The name of the company was changed to Kumardhubi Metal Casting and Engineering Limited (KMCEL). The company resumed its regular production in October 1984 under the new management. How was the revival of the company accomplished within a period of less than one year?

Key Problems

When erstwhile KEW was at its peak performance and making profits from its two divisions – Casting and Rolling Mill Divisions, a decision was taken to further enhance its profitability by investing in

---

* This case is based on the paper entitled 'Rehabilitation — Experience and Problems' presented by M.M. Sinha, Chairman, Kumardhubi Metal Casting and Engineering Limited (KMCEL) at a National Seminar on 'Industrial Sickness', November 22-23, 1985 organised by Management Development Institute, Gurgaon.

TABLE 10.1: Financial Profile of Kumardhubi Engineering Works Ltd.

(*Rs. in lakhs*)

	Year ending November				March (16 months)	Year ending March				
	1967	1968	1969	1970	1972	1973	1974	1975	1976	1977
Sales	178	242	215	456	762	452	441	693	466	666
Operating Expenses	182	206	215	421	678	410	399	624	513	667
Depreciation	10	11	11	10	17	14	15	18	20	25
Operating Profit	(−14)	25	(−11)	25	67	28	27	51	(−67)	(−26)
Earnings before Interest and Taxes	(−12)	27	(−10)	30	76	35	46	114	20	(−14)
Interest	19	21	23	24	34	24	26	34	38	43
Net Profit/Loss	(−31)	6	(−33)	6	42	11	20	80	(−18)	(−57)
Profit Retained	(−31)	6	(−33)	6	27	(−2)	13	80	(−18)	(−57)
Equity Share Capital	65	65	65	77	77	77	87	87	87	87
Preference Capital	12	12	12	12	12	12	27	27	27	27
Net Worth	130	136	102	118	145	144	182	262	203	187
Long Term Debt	59	59	59	59	254	61	61	61	51	86
Current Liabilities	315	358	362	392	171	328	348	359	448	591
Total Tangible Assets	504	553	543	565	572	533	591	682	703	864
Current Assets	291	341	342	359	317	260	324	380	398	469
Defensive Assets	141	168	150	168	152	91	106	161	164	218
Net Working Capital	(−24)	(−17)	(−40)	(−33)	146	(−68)	(−24)	21	(−50)	(−122)
Inventories	150	173	192	191	165	169	218	219	234	251
Debtors	91	120	105	122	108	84	101	155	115	164
Cash & Bank Balances	5	3	1	2	3	3	2	3	5	7
Market Value of Equity Shares of (Rs. 3 per Share) High (Rs.)	4.50	3.06	3.82	3.69	5.00	5.37	5.12	4.19	3.40	2.56
Low (Rs.)	2.25	2.03	2.37	2.00	3.37	3.19	3.00	2.94	1.75	1.47

Source: The Stock Exchange Official Directory, Bombay.

TABLE 10.2: Financial Viability Parameters of Kumardhubi Engineering Works Ltd.
(*Rs. in lakhs*)

Year ending	Net profit/loss	Cash profit/loss	Net working capital	Net worth
November				
1967	−31	−21	−24	130
1968	6	17	−17	136
1969	−33	−22	−40	102
1970	6	16	−33	118
March				
1972	31	44	146	145
1973	11	25	−68	144
1974	20	35	−24	182
1975	80	98	21	262
1976	−18	2	−50	203
1977	−57	−32	−122	187

TABLE 10.3: Health Score of Kumardhubi Engineering Works Ltd.
(*Multivariate Approach*)

Year ending	EBIT/TTA	CF/TTA	CA/CL	NS/TTA	DA/TOE	Health Score*	
						y_1	y_2
November							
1967	−.24	−.042	.923	.353	.779	.152	.317
1968	.048	.031	.952	.437	.815	1.666	1.478
1969	−.018	−.041	.944	.396	.697	.267	.303
1970	.053	.028	.915	.807	.399	1.828	1.428
March							
1972	.099	.076	1.853	.999	.299	2.835	2.046
1973	.065	.046	.792	.848	.221	2.008	1.584
1974	.045	.059	.931	.746	.265	1.559	1.718
1975	.074	.143	1.073	1.016	.258	2.327	3.17
1976	−.095	.003	.888	.663	.319	−1.257	.876
1977	−.030	−.037	.794	.771	.327	.185	.396

* (1) MDA Model for predicting industrial sickness
y_1 = 19.8927 EBIT/TTA + .0047 CA/CL + .7141 NS/TTA + .4860 DA/TOE
(Yadav, R.A., 'Financial Ratios and The Prediction of Corporate Failure', p.88).

(2) MDA Model for appraising the effectiveness of Working Capital Management
y_2 = 14.5166 CF/TTA + .0015 CA/CL + .8751 NS/TTA + .7914 DA/TOE
(Yadav, R.A., 'Working Capital Management – A Parametric Approach', *The Chartered Accountant*, May 1986).

steel making facilities and primary rolling facilities. Like any progressive management it was thought prudent to make the operation of the company independent of raw material supply from outside integrated steel plants and primary rollers of big ingots.

A plan was made to invest Rs. 200 lakhs in setting up a 10/12-T Arc Furnace and a 22″ rolling mill which could handle 7″ 8″, 8″ 9″ ingots produced from the arc furnace. In 1977 the expansion was completed after commissioning both the units. Against the set norms for financial discipline, working capital was diverted to meet the immediate requirement of capital investment. Due to shortage of working capital it became difficult to sustain normal operation of the plant. Mobilising advances against orders from the customers could continue the operation for short time only. The vicious circle so created brought the operations in both the divisions to a grinding halt in September 1979 and the management collapsed totally.

Financial problem enumerated above, though, was the main reason in the closer of the unit, chaos in the management, technical indiscipline followed by go slow tactics and general indiscipline, workers strike, demand recession, leading to idle capacity, lack of orders and uneconomic prices, scarcity of steel etc. also hastened the deteriorating conditions leading to closure.

Key Revival Strategies and Actions

The revival strategies followed by the company are explained below:

1. *Management Change*

In August 1984 TISCO management moved in Kumardhubi which was closed for about 5 years. The entire sheeting of the plant was corroded and quite a good number of them were hanging in dangerous condition. The elements had played havoc with the equipment. Most of them were sub-merged under water. Out of 31 EOT cranes none were in working order. All brass and copper parts of cross bars, current collectors, bearings, etc. were stolen. There was not a single piece of equipment which could be started as it is.

Rainy season being on, priority was given to roof sheeting which started immediately in the priority units where the operations were to start immediately. 12″ rolling mill and 2-T electric furnace were kept on top most priority. The mill had a number of auxiliary equipments where all the driving electrical units had practically zero insulation. In and around Kumardhubi there were not enough facilities which could take up the job of overhauling/repair of these electrical equipments. On crash basis facilities were rigged up at site itself with the available manpower augmented by few outside skilled workers. In about a month's time about 40 metres, a number of starters, control transformers, etc. were overhauled and made ready. Opening the units from foundation, transporting them to the overhauling site, getting them ready and fixing back on the foundation were done in a record time. The trial operation in the mill started in September 1984. In October 1984 the regular production in the mill was resumed. A strange coincidence occurred because of the assassination of the then Prime Minister on the 31st October, 1984. TELCO supply of spring flats were totally cut off from Punjab. It was 12″mill of KMCEL which started the rolling of spring flats, established the quality operation, and continued quality spring steel flats supply to TELCO thereby avoiding interruption in the truck manufacture at Jamshedpur and generating funds badly needed for KMCEL's revival. Close on the heels of this successful operation of 12″ Mill, the 18″ Mill was started in November 1984 producing a very profitable section of 30 Lb. Rails which further helped in generation of funds. In foundry 2-T furnace was started in the month of November 1984 and production of steel castings was resumed.

While all attention was paid to rehabilitation of plant and equipment, close watch was kept on units which could be made productive immediately and thereby earn substantial revenue for the sick unit.

2. *Financial Restructuring*

Management realised that for rehabilitation and operation of sick unit, mobilisation of the funds had to be given priority. Funds easily obtainable was of the share money for which all formalities were completed promptly and the share money was obtained from Bihar State Industrial Development Corporation and Tata Steel. Simultaneously the discussions started with Industrial Reconstruction Bank of India (earlier known as Industrial Reconstruction Corporation of India). After completing all the formalities a loan of Rs. 225 lakhs was sanctioned in less than 6 months' time., Working capital arrangement was made with Bank of India for a value of Rs.

150 lakhs. To minimise demand on working capital, 80 per cent production of the mill was arranged on conversion basis, raw material coming from an integrated Steel Plant.

3. *Human Resource Management*

(a) *Industrial Relations*

Besides the financial policy the management paid attention to a healthy industrial relations policy. The management believed that an industry can grow fast and come out of sickness only if the morale of the workers, supervisors and officers is kept high. It was only because of the firm belief, although the Kumardhubi Engineering Works (KEW) (Takeover and Management) Act had provided for payment to the workers the same salary as they were getting in 1979, the management doubled the amount of payment and brought them not only at par with the prevalent wage in the area but gave them Rs. 100 more. Although this being a new unit under totally a new management, exemptions could be obtained from Provident Fund Contribution, Annual Bonus, etc. but the management did not go for all this, instead agreed to pay 8.33 per cent Annual Bonus, started the Provident Fund deductions right from the beginning. The medical facilities availed with E.S.I. in that area is very disappointing. There is lot of dissatisfaction among all the workers of all industries in that area.

Management has taken up with the appropriate authority for exempting KMCEL from E.S.I. so that an independent hospital facilities can be set up by KMCEL for their workers.

(b) *Labour Relations*

Although management had taken steps to ensure satisfaction of the work-force, it was felt necessary to open a channel of communication for any grievances which might arise during the course of operation. For this, the leaders of the earlier union, who were interested in establishing their leadership more than the welfare of the workers, were not encouraged. Instead, all the workers employed were asked to elect their representatives from different sections. Thus a Workers' Council consisting of 8 members was formed among 1,200 workers employed. This Workers' Council meets once in a month or even more depending upon the need and it is functioning satisfactorily. Besides taking up the grievances they also discuss production, productivity and other problems of the works.

In spite of scarce funds position the management had spent substantial amount in improving the living conditions and sanitation in the Workers' Colony. Also provided drinking water facility which was not there earlier. Besides, a number of cultural programmes, children sports, etc. also were organised.

(c) *Discipline*

While giving benefits to the workers, management demanded two things from them – Production and Productivity and Discipline.

Right from the beginning punch clock system was introduced which the earlier management could not start in face of resistance from the workers. Strict gate control was enforced. Tea timings were fixed and it was ensured that people are on the work place always. Unruly elements were timely and properly dealt with. Positive behaviour among the workers was encouraged. To spread safety consciousness a number of safety activities were organised. Unsafe working conditions and practices were identified and they are being attended to systematically. The company has become a member of the Safety First Association of India and under their guidance a competent Senior Safety Officer is functioning effectively.

The entire revival operations of KMCEL is summarised as under:

1. A dedicated team of management personnel were deputed at Kumardhubi. They consisted of persons of proven ability in their respective fields who worked with zeal and enthusiasm round the clock under strenuous living conditions of camp life.
2. From among the available workers first set of workers were employed within a fortnight of the start of operation after observing all legal formalities.
3. For rehabilitation and subsequent operation all materials were moved at site promptly. The job was started in full swing within a month.
4. The units which could be rehabilitated with minimum effort for start of economic operation were attended to first.
5. Labour and welfare activities which appeared to be non-productive were given due importance to keep up the

morale of the work-force.

6. Share capital money to the tune of over a crore was mobilised in less than a month's time.
7. Loan application giving all the details was filed in three months' time and after vigorous follow-up the loan was sanctioned in next three months' time.
8. Working capital arrangement was made immediately when needed.
9. Working capital requirement was minimised by going for conversion arrangement.
10. Legal formalities of factory licence, industrial licence for different products, licence for storing fuel oil from Controller of Explosives, Weighbridge Certification, Excise Formalities, Sales Tax Registration, Railway Siding, etc. were all mostly completed in about four month's time inspite of many odds and bad legacy of the previous management.
11. Aggressive marketing was started for steel castings and help was taken for marketing of the rolled sections from the sales organisation of The Tata Iron and Steel Company Limited.

All the above had been possible because of vast resources of *Tata Steel* which was made available for this stupendous task. KMCEL management had liberally drawn heavily on *Tata Steel* technical expertise, material, machinery and their good will. Help was also available from different Government agencies, customers, etc.

APPENDIX

RESERVE BANK OF INDIA'S GUIDELINES FOR RELIEFS AND CONCESSIONS TO SICK UNITS, NOVEMBER, 1985

Viability

At the outset it must be emphasised that viability on a commercial basis should be the main criterion for undertaking the rehabilitation of a sick unit. This proposition should be adopted for identifying units to be put on a rehabilitation package. For this purpose viability is defined as under:

> A unit may be regarded as viable if it would be in a position, after implementing a relief package spread over a period not exceeding seven years from the commencement of the package, from banks, financial institutions, Government (Central/State), Government agencies, shareholders, labour, suppliers of goods and services and other creditors, as may be necessary, to continue to service its repayment obligations as agreed upon including those forming part of the package, without the help of the concessions after the aforesaid period. The repayment period for restructured debts should not exceed *ten years from the date of implementation of the package.*

I. Reliefs and Concessions on Existing Outstandings as also Sharing of Cash Losses

(i) *Term loans*

Interest on *term loans may be reduced* where considered necessary, *by not more than two per cent below* the prevailing rate, by both banks and term lending institutions, within this range of two per cent, however, the extent of reduction by the banks and the term lending institutions need not necessarily be equal. Any further reduction would require the Reserve Bank's prior clearance in respect of term loans from banks.

(ii) *Irregularity in cash credit account*

The irregular portion of the cash credit account may be segregated with reference to the first date of the accounting year from which the unit started incurring cash losses continuously.

(a) *Penalty and Damages*
Since the financial structure of sick units would already be distorted, levy of penal rate of interest or damages would further aggravate their problems. It would, therefore, be necessary to waive penalties and damages applied in the cash credit account.

(b) *Funded Interest*
It is usual for the packages to make a provision for segregating and funding the unrealised bank interest debited to the cash credit account (which is one of the factors rendering the account irregular). *The normal period of repayment of such funded interest should be 3 to 5 years.* In exceptional cases, this period could be elongated to 6 to 7 years at the discretion of the banks and term lending institutions. As funded interest is generally on a clean basis (i.e., unsecured) and will bear a rate of interest well below the normal rate on cash credit (please see sub-paragraph below), banks may ensure as far as possible that the *repayment of funded interest gets precedence over, or is spread over a shorter duration* than, the repayment of institutional loans.

> Funded interest should not be free of interest. Interest may be charged on funded interest at the rate of *10 per cent* subject to annual review. Where a lower rate of interest is felt necessary in exceptional cases it should be referred to the Reserve Bank for prior approval. Since a drastic reduction would affect the profitability of banks, their specific concurrence to the reduction envisaged in the package would be necessary. There will normally be no write off. Exceptional cases where write off is considered absolutely unavoidable, should be referred to the Reserve Bank.

(c) *Working Capital Term Loan (WCTL)*
The irregular portion of cash credit, other than unadjusted interest (on both cash credit and institutional loans) and after excluding penal interest/damages should be converted into a working capital term

loan (WCTL) with a definite repayment schedule. Interest shall be charged on the WCTL at a rate ranging between *15 per cent and 13.5 per cent*.

(d) *Sharing of Cash Losses*
The interest portion representing interest on term loans and working capital facilities should be segregated from the irregularity in the cash credit account. The interest portion so segregated should be funded, as pointed out earlier, and borne by the bank/s or institution/s, according to their respective shares. The remaining irregularity after segregating the interest portion as above would represent the cash loss of the unit already borne by the bank. Past cash losses would be normally reflected not only in the irregularity in the cash credit accounts of the banks, but also in non-payment of statutory dues, workers' dues and overdue creditors. Further, cash losses are also likely to be incurred during the initial period of implementation of the rehabilitation programme till the unit reaches the break-even level. Past cash losses, as reflected in the irregularity in the cash credit account, would have to be funded separately into a Working Capital Term Loan and should be borne by the banks themselves. The cash inputs required for meeting a part of overdue statutory liabilities, workers' dues and pressing creditors forming part of the package may be shared between the participating banks and institutions on 50: 50 basis. Future cash losses, i.e., losses from the time of implementation of the package up to the point of cash break-even as projected, would be borne by the financial institutions which will also provide the margin money for additional working capital. In cases where no term-lending institutions are already involved, the cash inputs mentioned above as also the projected cash losses would be borne/shared by the Industrial Reconstruction Bank of India. Thus, all cash inputs required for revival of the unit, other than those that will be shared with the banks as set out above, and in addition, future cash losses up to the point of break-even as projected in the rehabilitation package, will be taken care of by the concerned term lending institutions/IRBI. Additional cash losses arising on account of any deviation from the projections accepted in the package will be shared in an agreed manner as may be decided at the time of review of the package.

2. Additional Assistance

(i) *Need-based Working Capital*

Besides the funding of the existing irregularity in the accounts, need-based working capital would require to be provided to sustain further operating requirements of the unit. The requirements for working capital must be worked out strictly according to norms relating to inventory and receivables and should not exceed the permissible bank finance as computed under Method I, as far as sick units are concerned. Interest on working capital should be charged at the commercial rate, viz., between 16.5 per cent and 17.5 per cent at present, and the package should be prepared taking into account the rate of interests currently being charged by the banks. However, wherever concessions are forthcoming from the State Government, the banks may reduce the rate of interest to 15 per cent where necessary.

In order that there is no delay in the implementation of the package due to non-release of working capital funds, in cases where State Governments are willing to extend assistance, banks may release their share on getting a firm commitment from them regarding their contribution towards the reliefs and concessions, *provided the agreed contribution of promoters is forthcoming.*

(ii) *Pressing creditors*, and
(iii) *Statutory liabilities*

As indicated earlier, the term lending institutions, while determining the long term requirements in the package, will make adequate provision to meet the payments to pressing creditors such as suppliers of goods, that may be necessary to ensure continued availability of supplies on reasonable terms so that the operations of the unit are not hampered. These will be shared by the banks and institutions, or borne by the institutions as the case may be, as set out under item I(ii)(d) above.

(iv) *Start-up expenses*, and
(v) *Margin money*

These two items will be borne by the term lending institutions, as indicated earlier.

(vi) *Cost of rationalisation of labour*

This should be shared between the banks and term lending institutions on a 50-50 basis.

3. Time Span

As may be seen from the definition of viability given earlier, the period of rehabilitation packages should have an outer limit of seven years. If, within the framework of the parameters for concessions and reliefs as indicated above, a unit cannot be *expected to regain healthy within seven years,* then it should not be regarded as commercially viable. Where a unit is considered viable and a rehabilitation package has been drawn up, the period of repayment of restructured debts may, however, extend up to a maximum period of ten years. The rehabilitation package should invariably provide for the right of annual review of the reliefs and concessions extended.

4. Promoters' Contribution

Promoters' contribution should comprise fresh injection of funds as distinct from internal generation and proceeds from sale of assets already charged. Proceeds from sale of assets not charged, may be taken into account as promoters' contribution. In the cases involving change of management and professional management, the promoters should be required to bring in 15 per cent of the additional long term requirements envisaged under the package. In other cases, the *promoters' contribution shall be 20 per cent of the above, at least 10 per cent or 5 per cent as the case may be, within six months.* Such funds will be no *non-interest bearing basis.* If there is a indication that there has been-siphoning off of funds from the unit by the promoters/management, the package should stipulate that these funds should be brought back within a specified time limit. If this is not complied with, the further implementation of the package should be reviewed by the banks and term lending institutions.

5. RBI Approval

So long as the packages are drawn up within the framework of the parameters indicated above, the prior approval of the Reserve Bank will not be required. The details of package evolved should be reported to the Reserve Bank where the units enjoy working capital limits of Re. 1 crore and above from the banking system.

Only in cases where it is felt that concessions larger than those envisaged in these guidelines might be required to be provided to rehabilitate a unit on account of the already substantial involvement of banks/institutions, a reference should be made to the Reserve Bank of India, when the matter would be examined with reference to the special circumstances of the case vis-a-vis the prevailing policy.

As per fresh guidelines issued by the RBI to scheduled commercial banks, the present system of prior approval by the RBI for extending reliefs and concessions beyond the parameters fixed by it has been withdrawn for the grant of reliefs and concessions as part of the packages evolved for the rehabilitation of sick and weak units (*Economic Survey, 1990-91* p. 53).

6. Right of Recompense

In regard to concessions and reliefs made available to sick units, a clause could be added whereby, when the units turn the corner and the rehabilitation is successfully completed, the sacrifices undertaken by the institutions and banks should be recouped from the companies out of their future profits/cash accruals. Alternatively, there may be provision for equity participation to the extent of the sacrifices made.

7. Reliefs and Concessions from other Agencies

It should be ensured that the burden of reliefs and concessions is not borne by the banks and term lending institutions alone but is shared in an equitable manner by the various agencies interested in the revival of the units. An indicative list of the reliefs and concessions from other agencies such as State/Central Government, management and labour, which may be sought as part of the package, is given below:

An Indicative List of Reliefs and Concessions from other Agencies which may be sought as Part of the Packages

(1) *State Government*

(a) Sales tax loans should be provided at nil or very low rate of interest.

(b) State Government guarantee should be made available where needed for fresh advances.

(c) Preferential treatment should be given to sick industrial units in respect of power supply. Exemptions from power cuts should be made available for sick units.

(d) Power supply should not be cut unilaterally to sick industrial units when they are under a process of rehabilitation, if the electricity dues are not paid in time. A realistic rescheduling of such dues should be worked out.

(e) Exemption of certain concessions in the rate of sales tax, octroi duty and other duties/levies of the State/quasi-Government bodies should be given.

(f) Speedier disposal of industrial disputes should be ensured. Where the rehabilitation schemes envisage rationalisation of labour, State Governments should use their good offices in the matter. Where in the larger interest of rehabilitation of sick industrial units closure of one or more units forms part of the package, expeditious permission for closure as required under the I (D & R) Act should be given.

(g) Adequate market support for the products by strengthening the infrastructure should be provided.

(h) Banks and financial institutions should not be asked to stand guarantees for the payment of dues of the sick industrial units to the State/quasi-Government bodies.

(i) In respect of sick industrial units taken over by the State Governments, adequate budgetary support should be made to strengthen their equity base. Alternatively, State Industrial Development Corporation and State Industrial Investment Corporations might provide the requisite support.

(j) Penal levies in respect of sick industrial units should be waived as a part of the package.

(k) Declaration of sick industrial units as Relief Undertakings under the various States Relief Undertakings Acts may be made as a matter of course. Banks and term lending institutions should be exempted from the applicability of the Relief Undertakings Order.

(l) Price reference in the matter of purchases as given to public sector industrial units should be given.

(m) Expeditious permission under the Urban Land Ceiling Act, not only for creation of mortgage but also for sale of the mortgaged assets or excess vacant land to meet a part of the rehabilitation, should be given.

(n) Equity contribution should be provided wherever necessary, even where the units are not taken over by the State Government.

(II) *Central Government*

(a) Exemption from Central Excise, wholly or partly, for a period of time/deferment of collection or treating the dues as a loan repayable on the lines of sales tax loans from the State Government.

(b) Income-tax relief to banks in respect of amounts placed in Interest Suspense Account.

(c) Preferential allotment of canalised items to sick industrial units.

(d) Deferment of provident fund/waiver of penalties, income-tax and Employees' State Insurance dues and collection after suitable rephasing and ensuring at the same time that there is no deprivation of benefits to the retiring or sick employees.

(e) Exemption from payment of minimum bonus under the Payment of Bonus Act for a limited period, though the amount may continue to form a contingent liability to be discharged when the sick industrial unit is in a position to do so.

(f) Banks and financial institutions should not be asked to issue guarantee cover to the Central Government in respect of their dues, e.g., provident fund, income tax, excise duty and import duty.

(g) In respect of sick public sector undertakings, or 'defence oriented' sick industrial units which, in spite of their non-viability, Government wants to be assisted on considerations of public interest, budgetary support through equity or interest-free loans should be provided.

(h) Adequate marketing support should given to sick industrial units, if necessary, by reserving a certain quota for a certain period for purchase by Government/Semi-Government organisations. The sick industrial units should also be given price preference in the same way as public sector industrial units, as a measure of package.

(III) *Concessions and Sacrifices from the Management*

(a) Waiver or reduction of remuneration.
(b) Foregoing interest on any unsecured loans/deposits by self or friends and relatives.
(c) Write-off of loans.
(d) Bringing in fresh funds as may be decided under the package.
(e) Agreeing to reconstitution of management at the Board or operational level.
(f) Agreeing to appointment of finance/commercial directors/ controllers and concurrent auditors.
(g) Agreeing to provide personal guarantees/pledge of shares.
(h) Agreeing to discipline envisaged as part of the package.

(IV) *Concessions and Sacrifices from Labour*

(a) Voluntarily agreeing to schemes of rationalisation.
(b) Deferring or phasing out retrenchment compensation.
(c) Wage stabilisation, if not reduction, without agreeing on increases.
(d) Agreeing not to make any fresh demands for the specified period.
(e) Agreeing to increasing productivity and productivity linked incentives.

8. The RBI has also issued instructions that no single agency should unilaterally withdraw concessions/reliefs extended to a unit unless this has been agreed upon by all concerned. Banks were also advised that they should not lag behind in implementing their part of the obligations assumed under the rehabilitation packages for sick units.

9. As part of a package of measures for combating industrial sickness the government have announced in October 1989, a scheme for excise relief for weak industrial units. The scheme applies to any

industrial company, [excluding an ancillary industrial undertaking as defined in Section 3 of the Industrial (Development and Regulation) Act, 1951)] whose accumulated losses, at the end of any financial year, have resulted in erosion of 50 per cent or more of its maximum net worth during the immediately preceding 5 financial years. Such of these units as approved by an Empowered Committee constituted by the Central Government for a rehabilitation package will be eligible for grant of excise loan not exceeding 50 per cent of the excise duty actually paid for 3 years subsequent to the date of such approval. The total amount of excise loan shall not, in any case, exceed 25 per cent of the overall cost of the rehabilitation package. The excise loan will be interest free and is repayable within 7 years in instalments after a moratorium of 3 years commencing from the date of last disbursement of the loan. The scheme will be implemented through designated financial institutions like IDBI, IFCI, ICICI and IRBI). The scheme was further liberalised in september 1990 for sick industrial units employing more than 1000 workers and recommended by the BIFR for excise relief as part of an approved rehabilitation package. These units will be eligible for excise loan not exceeding 50 per cent of the excise duty actually paid for 5 years from the date of approval of the rehabilitation package subject to a ceiling of 33 per cent of the total cost of the rehabilitation (*Economic Survey, 1990-91*; p. 53).

9. Banks have been advised that the inter-se agreement among banks financing a healthy unit under consortium arrangement should provide for a clause to the effect that in case the unit turns sick, banks would be required to participate in the rehabilitation package in accordance with the instructions issued by the RBI.

10. In the case of sick units where workers are interested in taking over the management by forming Workers' co-operatives, banks have been advised to actively support the rehabilitation packages.

11. While banks have been advised by the RBI, time and again, that they cannot dissociate themselves from rehabilitation of sick/weak industrial units, they are now given the option of selling their debts in respect of a sick unit to other willing banks at a discount as per the guidelines issued by the RBI.

12. It has been decided that existing/additional facilities provided to sick/weak units under rehabilitation packages could be exempt from the application of the existing ceilings prescribed under the prudential norms of single group exposure limits.

BIBLIOGRAPHY

BOOKS

Allsop, M. (1977), *Survival In Business : The Dynamics of Success and Failure*, London : McGraw-Hill.

Altman, E.I. (1971), *Corporate Bankruptcy in America*, Lexington Mass., D.C. Heath and Co.

Altman, E.I. (1983), *Corporate Financial Distress : A Complete Guide to Predicting, Avoiding and Dealing with Bankruptcy*, Wiley.

Altman, E.I. and Arnold, W.S. (1977), *Financial Crisis Institutions and Markets in a Fragile Environment*, John Wiley and Sons, New York.

Andrews, Kenneth (1971), *The Concept of Corporate Strategy*, Homewood, Dow Jones Irwin.

Argenti, John (1976), *Corporate Collapie – The Causes and Symptoms*, McGraw-Hill, London.

Baramash, Isadore (1973), *Great Business Disasters*, Ballantine Books.

Bibeault, D.B. (1982), *Corporate Turnaround : How Managers Turn Losess into Winners*, McGraw-Hill, New York.

Bidani, S.N. and Mitra, P.K. (1983), *Industrial Sickness: Identification and Rehabilitation*, Vision Books, New Delhi.

Clutterbuck, D. and Kernaghan, Sue (1990), *The Phoenix Factor : Lessons for Success from Management Failure*, Werdenfeld and Nicolson, London.

Deeson, A.F.L. (1972), 'Great Company crashes', W. Foulsham.

Drucker, Peter (1980), *Managing in Turbulent Times*, Harper and Row, New York.

Eisenberg Joseph (ed.) (1972), *Turnaround Management : A Manual for Profit Improvement and Growth*, McGraw-Hill, New York.

Eisenberg, Joseph (ed.) (1972), *Turnaround Management: A Manual for Profit Improvement and Growth*, McGraw-Hill, New York.

Foster, George (1978), *Financial Statement Analysis*, Prentice-Hall Inc. New Jersey.

Fruchter, B., *Introduction to Factor Analysis*, D. Van Nostrand Company, Inc.

Glueck, William F. (1972), *Business Policy: Strategy Formulation and Executive Action*, McGraw-Hill, New York.

Goodman, Stanley J. (1982), *How to Manage a Turnaround : A Senior Manager's Guide*, Macmillan Publishing Co. Inc., New York.

Government of India, *Sick Industrial Companies (Special Provisions) Act 1985.*

Gupta, L.C. (1983) *Financial Ratios for Monitoring Corporate Sickness*, Oxford University Press, New Delhi.

Harman, Harry H. (1977), *Modern Factor Analysis*, The University of Chicago Press.

Higgins, Lindley R. (1976), *Cost Reduction from A to Z*, McGraw-Hill, New York.

Iacocca, Lee (1984), *Iacocca : An Autobiography*, Toronto Books.

Kaveri, V.S. (1980), *Financial Ratios as Predictiors of Borrowers Health*, Sultan Chand and Sons, New Delhi.

Kaveri, V.S. (1983), *How to Diagnose, Prevent and Cure Industrial Sickness*? : *A Practical Approach*, Sultan Chand and Sons, New Delhi.

Khandwalla, P.N. (1989), *Effective Turnaround of Sick Enterprises (Indian Experience) : Text and Cases*, Commonwealth Secretariat, London.

Kharbanda, O.P. and Stallworthy, E.A. (1985), *Corporate Failure : Prediction, Panacea and Prevention*, McGraw-Hill.

Kharbanda, O.P. and Stallworthy, E.A. (1987), *Company Rescue : How to Manage a Company Turnaround*, Heinemann, London.

Kibel, H.R. (1982), *How to Turnaround a Financially Troubled Company*? McGraw-Hill.

Lev, Baruch (1974), *Financial Statements Analysis : A New Approach*, Prentice-Hall, New Jersey.

Luthar, P.C. (1987), *Effective Management – Lessons of Experience*, Allied Publishers, Ahmedabad.

Mishkin, William S. (1972), *Techniques in Corporate Reorganisation*, Presidents Publishing House, New York.

Nelson, R. and Clutterbuck, D. (eds.) (1988), *Turnaround : How Twenty well-known Companies came Back from the Brink*, Mercury Books, London, Division of W.H., Allen and Co.

Overall, John E. and Klett, James, C (1972), *Applied Multivariate Analysis*, McGraw-Hills.

Padaki, V. and Shanbhag, S. (eds.), (1984), *Industrial Sickness : The Challenge in Indian Textiles*, Ahmedabad : ATIRA.

Peter, Thomas J. and Waterman, R.H. (1982), *In Search of Excellence; Lessons from America's Best Run Companies*, Harper and Row, New York.

Robertson, Andrews (1973), *The Lesson of Failure*, MacDonald, London.

Ross, J.E. and Kami, M.J. (1973), *Corporate Management in Crisis : Why the Mighty Fall*, Englewood Cliffs, N.J.: Prentice-Hall.

Rummel, R.J. (1970), *Applied Factor Analysis*, Evanston, North Western University Press.

Scherr, Frederick C. (1989), *Modern Working Capital Management: Text and Cases*, Prentice-Hall, New Jersey.

Slatter, S. (1984), *Corporate Recovery : Successful Turnaround Strategies and their Implementation*, Harmondsworth, Middlesex: Penguin, London.

Slatter, S.D. (1974), *The Strategy of Cash: A Liquidity Approach to Maximising the Company's Profit*, London : Wiley.

Smith, K.V. and Gallinger, G.W. (eds.) (1988), *Readings on Short-term Financial Management*, West Publishing Company, New York.

Smith, K.V., (1974), *Management of Working Capital*, West Publishing Company, New York.

Smith, R.A. (1966), *Corporations in Crisis*, Doubleday.

Srivastava, S.S. (1984), *Management Information System and Computers*, Atma Ram and Sons, Delhi.

Srivastava, S.S. and Yadav, R.A. (1986), *Management and Monitoring of Industrial Sickness*, Concept Publishing Company, New Delhi.

Tennent, M. (1976), *Practical Liquidity Management*, Epping Gower Press.

Wilson, Richard M.S. (1975), *Handbook of Cost Control*, Wiley, New York.

Yadav, R.A. (1986), *Financial Ratios and the Prediction of Corporate Failure*, Concept Publishing Company, New Delhi.

PERIODICALS

Altman, E.I. (1968), Financial Ratios, Discriminant Analysis and the Prediction of Corporate Bankruptcy, *Journal of Finance*, September, pp. 589-09.

Altman, E.I.; Haldeman, R.G. and Narayanan, P. (1977), 'Zeta Analysis : A New Model to Identify Bankruptcy Risk of Corporations', *Journal of Banking and Finance*, Spring.

Argenti, J. (1977), 'Company Failure – Long-range Prediction is not Enough', *Accountancy*, August, pp. 46-52.

Argenti, John (1976), The Anatomy of Company Failure: The Classical Syndrome, *The Accountant*, May.

Arun Subramaniam (1987), 'Kamani Tubes: Workers mean Business', *Business India*, February 9-22, pp. 63-67.

Bayler, Harmon (1973), 'Planning for Cost Reductions', *Management Accounting*, Vol. 54, April, pp. 31-36.

Beaver, W.H. (1966), Financial Ratios as Predictors of Failures, *Empirical Research in Accounting Selected Studies*, 1966, Supplement to Vol. 4, *Journal of Accounting Research*, pp. 71-127.

Beaver, W.H. (1968), 'Alternative Accounting Measures as Predictors of Failures', *Accounting Review*, January, pp. 113-22.

Beaver, W.H. (1968), 'Market Prices, Financial Ratios and the Prediction of Failure', *Journal of Accounting Research*, 6 (Autumn), pp. 79-92.

Beaver, W.H., Kennelly, J.W. and Voss, V.M. (1968), Predictive Ability as a Criterion for the Evaluation of Accounting, *The Accounting Review*, 43 (October 1968).

Bertodo, R. (1990), 'Implementing a Strategic Vision, *Long Range Planning*, Vol. 23, No. 5, October, pp. 22-30.

Bhatnagar, Rakesh (1988), 'KTL : Sick Unit Workers Make History', *The Times of India*, September 12.

Bhattacharyya, S.K. (1989), 'Executing a Turnaround', *Business World*, February 1-14, pp. 13-14.

Blum, M. (1974), 'Failing Company Discriminant Analysis', *Journal of Accounting Research*, Spring, pp. 1-25.

Bureau of Public Enterprises (1990) : *Public Enterprise Survey 1985-86 to 1989-90*, Vol. I, Ministry of Industry, Government of India, New Delhi.

Chakravarty, P. (1983), 'Executives' Opinion on Industrial Sickness', *The Management Accountant*, 18(12), pp. 530-33.

Chakravarty, Prabir (1985), 'Revival of a Sick Industrial Unit – A Case Study of an Engineering of West Bengal', *The Management Accountant*, February, pp. 89-90, 93.

Chandran, N.B. (1987), 'Journey to Excellence by FACT', *Chemical Engineering World*, 22(10), October, pp. 51-58.

Cherian, Dilip (1984), 'How to Guarantee Failure', *Business India*, April 19-22, pp. 56-62.

Cochran, W.G. (1964), 'On the Performance of the Linear Discriminant Function', *Technometrics*, Vol. 6, May, pp. 179-90.

D.K. Pani (1983), 'Enfield : Reviving up Again', *Business India*, December 5-18, pp. 84-91.

David, Brown L. (1984), 'Effective Change Strategies for Public Enterprises : Lessons from Turnaround Cases', *Vikalpa*, Vol. 9, No. 2, April-June, pp. 97-112.

Deakins, E.B. (1972), 'A Discriminant Analysis of Predictors of Failures', *Journal of Accounting Research*, Vol. I, No. 10, Spring, pp. 167-79.

Deboshis Basu (1989), 'Can Metal Box be Rescued', *Business World*, February 1-14, pp. 46-47.

Desai, V.V. (1980), 'Rehabilitation of Sick Units', *The Chartered Accountant*, July, pp. 11-14.

Dharani, K. Pani (1989), 'Madras Fertilisers : The Turnaround', *Business India*, November 27 – December 10, p. 79.

Dholakia, Bakul H. (1989), 'Industrial Sickness in India : Need for Comprehensive Identification Criteria', *Vikalpa*, Vol. 114, No. 2, April-June, pp. 19-24.

Dilip Maitra (1988), 'The Jhawars : A Winning Touch', *Business India*, March 21 – April 3, pp. 65-68.

Donaldson, G. (1962), New Framework for Corporate Debt Policy, *Harvard Business Review*, Vol. 40, March-April, pp. 117-31.

Dutta, Ashok (1980), 'Revival of Sick Units', *The Chartered Accountant*, April, pp. 907-09.

Edminister, R.O. (1972), 'An Empirical Test of Financial Ratio Analysis for Small Business Failure', *Journal of Financial and Quantitative Analysis*, Vol. 7, March, pp. 1477-93.

Fernandez, A. and Shanker P., (1988), 'Kamani Tubes : Tightrope Walk ahead for Workers, *Business India*, October 31 – November 13, pp. 81-83.

Fisher, R.A. (1936), 'The Use of Multiple Measurements in Taxonomic Problems', *Annals of Eugencies*, No. 7, pp. 179-88.

Gaffen, H. and Henry, Moss (1975), 'Multiple Skills called on When the Question is Survival', *Journal of Accountancy*, October, pp. 102-05.

Ganpati, R. (1990), 'Industrial Sickness : Unfair Criticism of BIFR : Negligence by Banks; Limited Powers Hamper BIFR', Series of 3 Articles in *The Economic Times*, August 9, 10 and 11.

Garry Purrel (1989), 'Industrial Sickness : Primary and Secondary', *Economic and Political Weekly*, May 27, pp. 81-84.

Gopal, R. (1989), 'Turnaround of a Cable Company', *Long Range Planning*, 22(1), pp. 98-101.

Grinyer, Peter H.; Mayes, David and McKiernan, Peter (1990), 'The Sharpbenders : Achieving a Sustained Improvement in Performance', *Long Range Planning*, Vol. 23, No. 1, February, pp. 116-25.

Gupta, Sijoy (1990), 'ICIM's Comeback', *Business World*, January 17-30, pp. 62-71.

Hambrick, D.C. and Schecter, S.M. (1983), 'Turnaround Strategies for Mature Industrial Products Business Units', *Academy of Management Journal*, Vol. 26, No. 2, pp. 231-248.

Hegde, M. (1982), 'Western and Indian Models of Turnaround Management', *Vikalpa*, Vol. 7, No. 4, pp. 289-303.

Hofer, C. (1980), 'Turnaround Strategies', *Journal of Business Strategy*, Vol. I, No. 1, pp. 19-31.

Horrigan, J.O. (1965), 'Some Empirical Basis of Financial Ratio Analysis', *Accounting Review*, Vol. 40, pp. 558-68.

Ishizuna, Yasuhiro (1990), The Transformation of Nissan – The Reform of Corporate Culture, *Long Range Planning*, Vol. 23, No. 3, June, pp. 9-15.

Jain, M.P. (1987), 'JMEL : Trend Setter for Sick Units', *Business India*, February 23 – March 8, p. 79.

Jain, S.N. (1987), 'Turnaround Management Strategy', *The Economic Times*, January 20.

Joseph, Lancelot (1989), 'Special Steels: Back on the Rails', *Business India*, November 27 – December 10, pp. 74-77.

Kashyap, S.P. and Amita Shah (1989), 'Ailing Industrial System of India – A Diagnosis', *Economic and Political Weekly*, May 27, pp. 77-80.

Kaul, Mohan (1990), 'Public Enterprise Management : Strategies for Success', *Vikalpa*, Vol. 15, No. 1, January-March, pp. 3-13.

Khandwalla, P.N. (1981), 'Strategy for Turningaround Complex Sick Organisations', *Vikalpa*, Vol. 6, Nos 3 & 4, July & October, pp. 143-65.

Khandwalla, P.N. (1983), 'Turnaround Management in the Public Sector', *Lok Udyog*, September, pp. 25-37.

Khandwalla, P.N. (1986), 'Effective Turnaround Management', Series of 4 articles in *The Economic Times*, February 10, 11 and March 27, 28.

Khandwalla, P.N. (1988), 'What can Financial Institutions do to prevent Corporate Sickness', *Vikalpa*, Vol. 13, No. 2, April-June, pp. 11-23.

Khandwalla, P.N. (1991), 'Humane Turnarounds', *Vikalpa*, Vol. 16, No. 2, April-June, pp. 3-16.

Korgaonkar, M.G. (1987), 'Project Management: A Survey of Current Practices and Implications', *Vikalpa*, Vol. 12, No. 4, October- December, pp. 11-25.

Kotler, Philip (1965), 'Phasing out Weak Products', *Harvard Business Review*, March-April, pp. 109-16.

Kratchman, S.H.; Richard T.H. and Thomas A.U. (1975), 'Management's Decision to Discontinue a Product', *Journal of Accountancy*, June, pp. 50-54.

Kumar, K.G. (1988), 'Aluminium Industries (ALIND) Do or Die', *Business India*, June 13-16, pp. 61-67.

Kumar, K.G. (1988), 'The Fertilisers and Chemicals Travancore Limited', *Business India*, April 4-17, pp. 71-74.

Kumar, K.G. 'Appollo Tyres Limited : No more Skidding', *Business India*, June 13-16, pp. 61-67.

Laurant, L.R., (1979), Improving the Efficiency and Effectiveness of Financial Ratio Analysis, *Journal of Business Finance and Accounting*.

Madhumita Bose (1989), 'Metal Box India : Blind Man's Buff', *Business India*, March 6-19, pp. 73-76.

Madhumita Majumdar (1986), 'Guest Keen Williams : On the Road to Recovery', *Business India*, January 27-February 9, pp. 60-65.

Madhumita Majumdar (1988), 'Metal Box India : Will it Survive', *Business India*, January 11-24, pp. 60-63.

Ministry of Finance, *Economic Survey, 1984-85 to 1990-91.*

Mitra, Kaveri (1987), 'Guest Keen Williams : Reviving an Ailing Giant', *Business India*, December 14-27, pp. 51, 55; 'Flickering Fortunes', *Business India*, April 4-17, 1988, pp. 65-66' 'A Revival of Sorts', *Business India*, February 6-19, 1989, p. 97; GKW : Back from the Brink', *Business India*, September 3-16, pp. 85, 87.

Mittal, B.B. (1987), 'Revival of a Sick Unit: A Case Study', *The Chartered Accountant*, Vol. 36, No. 5, pp. 432-435.

Molin, L. (1985), Strategies in Managing Turnaround, *Long Range Planning*, Vol. 18, No. 1, pp. 80-86.

Morris, S. (1982), 'Why do Industries Turn Sick', *Business India*, November 22 – December 5, pp. 46-55.

Morrison, Donald D. (1969), 'On the Interpretation of Discriminant Analysis', *Journal of Marketing Research*, May.

Muller, R. (1985), Corporate Crisis Management, *Long Range Planning*, Vol. 18, No. 1, pp. 38-48.

Muller, R. (1985), 'Corporate Crisis Management', *Long Range Planning*, Vol. 18, No. 5, pp. 38-48.

Myer, P.A. and Pifer, H.W. (1970), 'Prediction of Bank Failures', *Journal of Finance*, Vol. XXV, Spring, pp. 853-868.

Natarajan, R.; Krishnamurthy, G. and Rao, K.V.J. (1985), 'Rehabilitation of Sick Units in SSI Sector through Marketing Strategy – A Case Study', *Indian Journal of Marketing*, Vol. 15, No. 7, pp. 13-16.

NLC : A Perennial Source of Thermal Power, *The Times of India*, May 31, 1985.

Norton, Curtis L. and Smith, Ralph E. (1979), 'A Comparison of General Price Level and Historical Cost Financial Statements in the Prediction of Bankruptcy', *The Accounting Review*, Vol. LIV, No. 1, January 1979, pp. 72-87.

O' Neill H.M. (1986), 'Turnaround and Recovery : What Strategy do You Need?', *Long Range Planning*, Vol. 19, No. 1, pp. 80-89.

Ohlson, James A. (1980), 'Financial Ratios and the Probabilistic Prediction of Bankruptcy', *Journal of Accounting Research*, Spring, pp. 109-31.

Padma Ramnath (1988), 'AFT : An Open Door Approach', *Business India*, October 31 – November 13, p. 149.

Padwal, S.M. and Bandopadhyay, R. (1977), 'Information System Design in a Commercial Bank', *Operational Research Quarterly*, Vol. 26.

Padwal, S.M. and Bandopadhyay, R. (1979), 'Concepts and Framework for Information', *Management Accountant*, February.

Pillai, K.R. (1985), 'Industrial Sickness Problems and Solutions', *The Economic Times*, December 28.

Pillai, P.K.N. (1984), 'Turningaround a Sick Unit – A Practical Approach', *The Economic Times*, June, 6.

Prabhu, Rajendra (1984), 'How Sick Units Regain Health', *The Hindustan Times*, September 24.

Prafull Anubhai (1988), 'Sickness in Indian Textile Industry', *Economic and Political Weekly*, November 26, pp. 147-57.

Prahlad Basu (1987), 'A Strategy for Public Enterprises Turnaround', *The Economic Times*, January 20.

Prahlad, C.K. and Thomas, P.S. (1977), 'Turnaround Strategy: Lessons from HPF's Experience', *Vikalpa*, Vol. 2, No. 2, April, pp. 99-111.

Prasad, N.S. (1982), 'Curing Sickness in Industries', *Indian Journal of Marketing*, Vol. 13, No. 3, pp. 19-22.

Rajagopal, S. (1989), 'Preventing Corporate Sickness : Improving the Working of Financial Institutions', *Vikalpa*, Vol. 14, No. 1, p. 65

Reserve Bank of India, Report on *Trend and Progress of Banking in India*, 1985-86 to 1989-90.

Reserve Bank of India, *Report on Currency and Finance*, 1984-85 to 1989-90.

Robertson, J. and Mills, R.W. (1988), 'Company Failure or Company Health : Techniques for Measuring Company Health', *Long Range Planning*, Vol. 22, No. 1, pp. 70-77.

Ruwe, D.M. and Skinner, W. (1987), 'Reviving a Rust Belt Factory', *Harvard Business Review*, May-June, pp. 70-77.

Schendel, D.E. and Patton, G.R. (1976), 'Corporate Stagnation and Turnaround', *Journal of Economics and Business*, Vol. 28, Spring, Summer, pp. 236-41.

Schendel, D.E.; Patton, G.R. and Riggs, J. (1976), 'Corporate Turnaround Strategies : A Study of Profit Decline and Recovery', *Journal of General Management*, Vol 3, No. 3, pp. 3-11.

Schoeffler, S., Robert D.B. and Donald F.H. (1971), 'The Impact of Strategic Planning on Profit Performance', *Harvard Business Review*, March-April, pp. 137-45.

Sharma, Rahul (1990), 'NELCO Seeking a Focus', *Business India*, September 3-16, pp. 73-75.

Sharma, Rahul (1990), 'Small is Better', *Business India*, July 23 – August 5, pp. 79-81.

Sijoy Gupta (1989), 'GKW Rises from the Ashes', *Business World*, September 27 – October 10, p. 95.

Sinha, M.M. (1985), 'Rehabilitation – Experience and Problems', Paper presented at a *National Seminar on Industrial Sickness*, November 22-23, MDI, Gurgaon.

Sorter, G.H. and Benston, G. (1960), 'Appraising the Defensive Position of a Firm : The Internal Measure', *Accounting Review*, October, pp. 633-40.

Srivastava, S.S. (1983), Management of Industrial Sickness, *Productivity*, October-December.

Starbuck, W.H.; Greve, A. and Hedberg B. (1978), Responding to crisis, *Journal of Business Administration*, pp. 111-78, Spring.

Stevenson, Howard H. (1976), 'Defining Corporate Strengths and Weaknesses', *Sloan Management Review*, Spring, pp. 51-67.

Subrata Roy (1983), 'Metal Box up for Sale', *Business India*, September 12-25, pp. 62-68; 'The Metal Box : The Macneill and Magor Stake', *Business India*, January 13-26, 1986, pp. 62-67.

Subrata Roy (1987), 'SAIL : Will it Succeed', *Business India*, August 10-23, pp. 42-52.

Subrata Roy (1990), 'GKW: Life after Death', *Business World*, July 18-31, pp. 38-41.

Sushila Ravindranath (1988), 'Enfield India : Riding Through Rough Times', *Business India*, March 7-20, pp. 73-75.

Swami, Parthasarthi (1988), 'The NELCO Turnaround', *Business World*, April 11-24, pp. 59-71.

Taffler, R. and Tishan, H. (1977), 'Going, Going, Gone – Four Factors which Predict Failure', *Accountancy*, March, pp. 50-54.

Tamari, M. (1966), 'Financial Ratios as Measure of Forecasting Bankruptcy', *Management International Review*, Vol. 4, pp. 15-21.

Taylor, B. (1982/1983), Turnaround, Recovery and Growth : The Way Through the crisis, *Journal of General Management*, Vol. 8, No. 2, pp. 5-13, Winter.

Taylor, Bernard (1983), 'Management of Turnaround and Recovery', *Productivity*, Vol. XXIV, 2, pp. 113-17.

Tithwal Mills Case, Parts A to F, *Indian Institute of Management*, Ahmedabad.

Travers, R.M.W. (1939), The Use of a Discriminant Function in Treatment of Psychological Group of Differences', *Psychometrica*, Vol. 4, No. 1.

Trivedi, Prajapati (1988), 'Public Enterprise Performance Information System : A Proposal', *Economic and Political Weekly*, November 26, pp. 140-46.

Turner, G. (1986), 'Inside Europe's Giant Companies : Oliveth Goes Bear-Hunting', *Long Range Planning*, Vol. 19, No. 2, pp. 13-20.

Vancil, Richard F. (1972), 'Better Management of Corporate Development', *Harvard Business Review*, September-October.

Vasuki, S.N. (1988), 'ICIM Uncertain at the Top', *Business India*, January 25 – February 7, pp. 79-81.

Vinay Kamath (1989), 'Enfield's Downmarket Push', *Business World*, October 25 – November 7, pp. 57-61.

Vinay Kamath (1990), 'The Anglo French Revival', *Business World*, February 28 – March 13, pp. 45-49.

Vittal, N. (1989), 'The Unusual Story of Gujarat Narmada Auto Ltd : A Case Study', *Management in Government*, Vol. 20, No. 4.

Walter, J.E. (1957), Determination of Technical Solvency, *Journal of Business*, January 31, pp. 30-43.

Walter, J.E. (1959), 'A Discriminant Function for Earnings Price Ratios of Large Industrial Corporation', *Review of Economics and Statistics*, Vol. XLI, February, pp. 44-52.

Whetton, D.A. (1980), 'Organisational Decline : A Neglected Topic in Organisational Science', *Academy of Management Review*, 5, pp. 577-88.

Whitney, John O. (1987), 'Turnaround Management Everyday', *Harvard Business Review*, September-October, pp. 49-55.

Wilcox, J.H. (1976), 'Gambler's Ruin Approach to Business', *Sloan Management Review*, Vol. 18, pp. 33-46.

Williams, Charles M. (1984), 'When the Mighty Stumble', *Harvard Business Review*, No. 62, July-August, pp. 126-39.

Yadav R.A. (1988), 'Detecting Industrial Sickness — A Multivarite Approach', *The Chartered Accountant*, November, pp. 468-73.

Yadav, R.A. (1986), 'Sick Industrial Companies Legislation – Remedy of the Palliative', *The Chartered Accountant*, Vol. 35, No. 6, pp. 289-92.

Yadav, R.A. (1986), 'Working Capital Management – A Parametric Approach', *The Chartered Accountant*, May, pp. 952-55.

Yadav, R.A. (1990), 'Assessing Health of Small Scale Industries – A System Approach', *MDI Management Journal*, Vol. 3, No. 2 July, pp. 99-110.

Yadav, R.A. (1990), 'Designing Management Information System for Monitoring Industrial Health', *ASCI Journal of Management*, Vol. 20, No. 7, June, pp. 1-13.

Yalawar, Yalaguresh B. and Iyer, Ramu P. (1984), 'Revival in Management Responsibility', *The Economic Times*, August, 3.

Yolamuresh, B., Yalawar and Ramu, P. Iyer (1984), Timely Assessment of Key Symptoms, *The Economic Times*, August 2.

Zimmerman, F.M. (1982), Turnaround – A Painful Process, *Long Range Planning*, Vol. 19, No. 4, pp. 104-14.

Zimmerman, F.M. (1989), 'Managing a Successful Turnaround, *Long Range Planning*, Vol. 22, No. 3, pp. 105-24.

'Rs. 1955 Crores for Neyveli Expansion', *The Economic Times*, June 30, July 14 and July 19, 1986.

INDEX